All Grown Up

All Grown Up

*Living Happily
Ever After
with Your
Adult Children*

ROBERTA MAISEL

NEW SOCIETY PUBLISHERS

Cataloguing in Publication Data:A catalog record for this publication is available from the National Library of Canada.

Cover design by Diane McIntosh. Cover photo: © (Gary Buss)/Getty Images/ FPG

Printed in Canada by Friesens.

New Society Publishers acknowledges the support of the Government of Canada through the Book Publishing Industry Development Program (BPIDP) for our publishing activities, and the assistance of the Province of British Columbia through the British Columbia Arts Council.

BRITISH
COLUMBIA
ARTS COUNCIL
Supported by the Province of British Columbia

Paperback ISBN: 0-86571-439-8

Inquiries regarding requests to reprint all or part of *All Grown Up* should be addressed to New Society Publishers at the address below.

To order directly from the publishers, please add $4.50 shipping to the price of the first copy, and $1.00 for each additional copy (plus GST in Canada). Send check or money order to:

New Society Publishers
P.O. Box 189, Gabriola Island,
BC V0R 1X0, Canada

New Society Publishers' mission is to publish books that contribute in fundamental ways to building an ecologically sustainable and just society, and to do so with the least possible impact on the environment, in a manner that models this vision. We are committed to doing this not just through education, but through action. We are acting on our commitment to the world's remaining ancient forests by phasing out our paper supply from ancient forests worldwide. This book is one step towards ending global deforestation and climate change. It is printed on acid-free paper that is **100% old growth forest-free** (100% post-consumer recycled), processed chlorine free, and printed with vegetable based, low VOC inks.

For further information, or to browse our full list of books and purchase securely, visit our website at:

NEW SOCIETY PUBLISHERS   www.newsociety.com

For Ben, Betsy, and Noah,
and for Bob, who was watching
over my shoulder.

Contents

Acknowledgments

THROUGHOUT THE WRITING of this book, my three adult children — Ben, Betsy, and Noah — have never been far from my consciousness. Their presence in my life has informed my ideas and has inspired me to harvest the riches embedded in our shared history. Accordingly, they are the subject of many of the stories and anecdotes in the book. I thank them for being the wonderful people that they are. Hey, guys, I'm proud of you.

My friend, Nicole Milner, announced one day that there seems to be a need for a book on parents and adult children, to which I responded, "Let's write one." She helped me greatly with earlier stages of *All Grown Up*.

Eric Maisel, author, brother-in-law, friend, and all-around publishing guru explained to me what a book proposal was — and a thousand other things, all wise and vital. He believed I could write this book and filled me with the confidence to take one step at a time, even when things looked dark.

Andy Langer got me out of endless computer glitches with uncomplaining and unhurried generosity. His patience with me was — how shall I say it? — a model of lovingkindness.

And my friend, Mort Levy, was kind enough to edit the entire manuscript with utmost graciousness and care.

I thank all of my interviewees, who gave of their time and shared their parenting stories with me — their ups and downs, the good times and the bad.

I thank the good people — staff and volunteers — at Berkeley Dispute Resolution Service who have provided me with a clear and useable model for minimizing conflict in everyday life.

Larry Vaughan and Susie Kaufman helped by reading and critiquing chapters.

Chris Plant and all the folks at New Society Publishers have been very open, supportive, and cooperative. Most of all, I thank them for taking a chance on me, a first-time author. I am deeply appreciative of their vision.

Introduction

THE EVOLUTION OF THIS BOOK was both distressing and deeply fulfilling: distressing because it evoked memories of the difficult hoops each of my three children had to jump through to reach adulthood. Further, it brought me face-to-face with my own mistakes. I have only recently, after some physical remove from all three of my adult children, begun to see the ways in which the good and the bad have blended to produce three lovely, imperfect, immensely human souls.

The fulfilling part came as I made contact with other midlife parents of adult children and discovered what they were experiencing. Were they communicating in ways that opened up the door to adult/adult relationships? Or were they exacerbating pockets of irritability and anger in their children — pockets that had been hanging around since early adolescence?

I listened to the stories of 25 parents — fathers and mothers in the 48- to 70-year-old range — as well as to those of a few adult children. These two to two-and-a-half hour taped interviews often evoked familiar feelings, though the content of the stories differed. Yes, I would think, I've been through that, too. I have had trouble embarking on a shared activity with an adult child. ("They are so busy; they have their own lives to lead," I would tell myself.) I, too, felt vaguely that it was my fault when one of my adult children was unhappy or unfulfilled.

Beyond the formal interviews, I found myself keeping an open mind and an attentive ear as I listened to friends and acquaintances. Over coffee or elongated lunches, midlife parents needed little encouragement to talk about their difficulties with their role as grandparents, about how hard it was for them not to give advice, or about how they sometimes felt neglected by their adult children. I also listened to my family members and tried to understand the implications of the increasingly common four-generation family configuration as a result of the new longevity. Once I caught my 92-year-old mother-in-law enjoying a moment of reflection: "Amanda is about to enter college," she noted. "I can't believe I have an 18-year-old great-granddaughter. With any luck, I'll have a great-great-grandchild."

1

It's true. Esther and my 93-year-old mother, Henrietta, are still spry and healthy, pushing along toward that fastest-growing segment of the population — those over a hundred years old. They and others like them are making it hard to find words to describe men and women in their 50s and 60s — those who used to be called "the older generation."

The first crop of baby boomers, people in their early 50s, are perhaps exemplified by Bill and Hillary Clinton: still vigorous, setting out on new roads and projects, and anticipating many good years ahead. Yet these fiftysomethings may have adult children who are in their 20s or 30s, as well as grandchildren.

A new population configuration is emerging. More and more we are seeing breakthroughs in disease prevention and cure that have pushed longevity statistics to unheard-of heights. A 62-year-old woman with no history of cancer or heart disease can be expected to live, on average, to 85. Many older people will be living productive, healthy, and pain-free lives into their 80s and beyond.

Although it is true that couples in a certain segment of the middle class have been having fewer and later babies, many parents who are 48 or 52 or 56 discover that, lo and behold, their children are grown! They're 25 or 29 or 32 and the world sees them as adults. But are they really? Are they on their own, able to cope, partnered, educated, settled into satisfying work, financially secure, and responsible?

"Whoa, wait a second," parents may say, "was I all those things at 30?" Probably not, though they might have finished their education, started their first serious job at 22, married at 27, and started a family at 29. After some reflection, parents may begin to regard the adulthood of their offspring as a debatable issue. In addition, their relationship to their adult children may be unclear: It's not one of equality but neither is it a caretaker relationship. What exactly is the midlife parent's role?

Gradually it became clear to me that all is not well between midlife parents and their grown children. As the planning and writing of this book evolved, my theme and my goal expanded and deepened. I set out to show that midlife parents can have a relationship with their adult children that is simultaneously a generational bond and an egalitarian friendship. I began to articulate a new model for the parenting of adult children in the new millenium.

1

GETTING TO KNOW EACH OTHER

The Parallel Worlds of
Parents and Adult Children

> "If there is anything that we wish to
> change in the child — see whether it is
> not something that could better be
> changed in ourselves."   — Carl Jung

MANY MIDLIFE PARENTS don't know how to parent their adult children. Indeed, they may not be sure that they need or want to parent at all — or whether their children need or want their parenting. Though it is difficult, possibly painful, to think about, they may not be sure that their grown children love them.

These issues are not merely academic. The practical realities of life often force parents to make difficult decisions around parental responsibility. Does a 60-year-old parent owe financial support, child care, occasional room and board, or down payment on a house to a 30-year-old "child"? Is there one right answer to this question? Are there guidelines to help us sift out the important from the trivial and make sensible decisions?

My oldest child, Ben, said to me a few years ago, "You know, Mom, it's hard being a teacher. You're on stage all the time and have to perform, either for the kids or the parents or both. You have no place to hide. And there's always someone who doesn't like you, who doesn't feel you're good enough."

I listened, shook my head in recognition, commiserated: I had been a teacher, too. But I also felt a wave of guilt wash over me. What had I done wrong as a parent? My son had been shy and sensitive as a boy, and still was at 35. What had I done way back; and what was I, perhaps, still doing now? Could I, should I, try to fix things? Where does a parent's responsibility end — or does it?

Novelist J.M. Coetzee observes the minutiae of the parent/adult child role in this passage from *Disgrace*: "He has stayed with his daughter only for brief periods before. Now he is sharing her house, her life. He has to be careful not to allow old habits to creep back, the habits of a parent: putting the toilet roll on the spool, switching off lights, chasing the cat off the sofa."[1] The habits of parents are so deeply ingrained that we don't (or can't) step back far enough to see them.

As I sought guidelines for parental involvement and responsibility, I knew I needed to define "adult" or "grownup." Surprisingly, I came up with four definitions. The legal meaning of adult refers to age: the age at which one can vote, can marry, can serve in the military, must suffer the full consequences of illegal behavior. These ages differ from country to country, and, within the United States, often from state to state. In some states one is deemed mature enough to marry at 15. At least in the context of ability to function as a husband or wife, one is therefore seen as an adult at 15.

My second definition of adult was very simple — primitive, even. When one is fully physically grown, usually between 19 and 21, one is literally grown up.

A third definition was more difficult to pin down but seemed meaningful nevertheless. It had to do with the age at which a person left school and was out in the world of work. Somehow a person working was more of a grownup than a person living off his or her parents. And yet... Numerous exceptions clouded my proposition, rendering it all but useless. Was a 17-year-old working full-time at an entry-level restaurant job more of an adult than a 29-year-old grad student struggling with a dissertation and living largely off parental bounty? Was there a point at which staying in school became malingering? Could a person be a grownup, though economically dependent, at 20? 25? 30? And what about handicapped people, for whom job opportunities were more limited? Defining adult was becoming complicated.

My fourth definition of adult struck out on a different path altogether. Its vital center was the concept of responsibility, the degree to which an individual made responsible decisions regarding herself and her loved ones. Responsibility was not always easy to define but one knew what it wasn't. It wasn't partying the night before an exam; it wasn't consistently arriving late for work; it wasn't forgetting to put the baby in the car seat. Using these criteria, some people never became grownups.

The social/economic world in which we are embedded colors our definition of adult, as does history. In past centuries, a Jewish boy of 13 was considered old enough to take on some of the responsibilities of manhood as spelled out in his Bar Mitzvah rite of passage. Indeed, he may have married and started to raise a family not long afterward. Life was short. Early procreation was mandatory if the tribe was to survive. Adolescence, not to mention extended adolescence, was unknown. The rite of passage into adulthood coincided with the onset of the ability to reproduce. This is still the case in many tribal societies today.

Even as recently as 50 years ago, defining adult was significantly less problematic than it is today. Upon leaving high school, an 18-year-old went on to college or got a job. If she went to college she generally completed it without a hiatus for working, traveling, or "finding herself." If she decided against college, she might take an entry level job, continuing to live with her parents in order to save money. In her mid-twenties she had a good chance of being able to afford her own small apartment.

Our hypothetical protagonist, furthermore, was programmed for marriage by her early or middle 20s. In the dark ages of the 1950s, the markers of adult status were almost universally agreed upon: finishing school, finding work or attending graduate school, achieving financial self-sufficiency, getting married and having children. A young person of 22 could easily be considered an adult.

The 1960s and '70s changed all that. People in their 20s and 30s experimented with many things, including putting off growing up. They turned marriage, parenting, and all manner of middle class values upside down. An unpopular war caused youth to question and condemn adults and adult values. People over 30 were not to be trusted. If you were under 30 — say, 25 — you were, mercifully, not yet adult.

The Roots of the Generation Gap

The legacy of the '60s and '70s has been colored by events following that period: the conservative backlash of the 1980s, the recessionary period of the early 1990s, the technology-driven economic growth of the late 1990s. Nevertheless, people in their 50s and 60s are still reeling from the awesome social changes that have taken place in their lifetime. They are trying to feel comfortable with social institutions which are staggeringly different from those of their childhoods and with which their 20- to 35-year-old children are quite at home.

Who are these young adults, our children, who don't remember a time before about 1963, when:

- an unmarried couple living together were considered to be living in sin;
- an unmarried mother was bad;
- an unmarried woman was labeled a spinster;
- women, if they did have careers, were expected to become school teachers, social workers, librarians, or domestic servants — not trombonists, soccer players, construction workers, or heads of state;
- single men and women did not share college dormitories;
- it was socially unacceptable for married couples to choose not to have children;
- gays and lesbians were almost totally in the closet.

All these changes in mores in barely forty years are reverberating through the social fabric, shaking things up that appeared solid and substantial. Those of us who grew up in the period before the 1960s are inhabiting a different world from the one our adult children inhabit.

Can we identify a single factor that brought on the sexual/feminist revolutions of the '60s and '70s? Was there one Big Bang that caused it all? Is it the same Big Bang that caused the loosening of prohibitions against homosexuals? What happened in the 20th century to make women in industrial/advanced countries move into uncharted waters — putting off marriage for decades while pursuing education and career, or choosing not to marry at all? If we can begin to understand what happened we may grasp the awesome rapidity of recent social change — and the consequent problems we face in trying to understand and live comfortably with our adult children.

Locating and describing the Big Bang, if indeed there is such, becomes less daunting if we focus on changing population statistics: in particular, longevity, infant and birth mother mortality, and the worldwide conquest of disease.

In 1850, average life expectancy at birth in the U.S. was 38.[2] This figure represented high infant mortality, for life expectancy shot up to 58 if calculated from the age of 10. One hundred years later, at-birth average life expectancy rose to 66, and in 1999, the most recent year for which statistics were available at this writing, average U.S. life expectancy at birth reached the unprecedented height of 78. Furthermore, in 1997, 60-year-olds had an average life expectancy of 83 for women and 78 for men, 85 and 82 if calculated from age 70.

In the 20th century, for the first time in human history, the pressure was off reproduction.

Changes in death rates are equally dramatic. Between 1900 and 1998, U.S. deaths per 1000 persons plummeted from 17.2% to 8.6%. Infant mortality statistics are also striking: Between 1950 and 1999 in the U.S., infant deaths per 1,000 live births went from 30 to 6, with similar low figures for other industrial nations: Japan (4), Israel (8), Canada (5), United Kingdom (6). There is every reason to believe these rates will continue to go down.

With the conquering of many killer diseases and the leap forward in longevity in the 20th century, the concept of zero population growth, and even negative population growth, entered our consciousness. In the 20th century, for the first time in human history, the pressure was off reproduction.

As recently as the early 18th century, Queen Anne of England was unable to produce an heir to the throne, though she gave birth to four children. With the best medical technology and wisdom of the time, three of them died in infancy or early childhood, and the fourth died in his teens. Stories like this can be replicated in the 19th century as well, with bloodletting still a major medical strategy and asepsis not yet taken seriously.

Today, pre-industrial or emerging nations (such as China, India, Indonesia) can't move fast enough to hold back reproduction. Women do not have to start bearing children at puberty and continue until menopause or death. Families do not have to bear as many children as they possibly can in order that a few of them might live to take care of their parents when they can no longer work.

Grandma Anna, my mother's mother, emigrated to the U.S. from Romania in about 1895 at the age of 20, with her mother and sister. She was a member of a white collar Jewish family, forced to leave due to a pogrom — what amounted to a massacre — that came down upon the town of Iassi where the family lived. Grandmother married in the States and gave birth to two children, a boy and a girl. She devoted her life to homemaking and child rearing and never worked out of the home. When her husband died of a misdiagnosed and mistreated illness at 40, the two children knew that they would be supporting their mother the rest of her life. My mother, still in high school, quickly switched from a college preparatory track to a business track and took a job as a legal secretary upon graduation. When my mother and father married in 1930 it was understood that Anna would be living with them until she died. She went to her daughter's home and not her son's because her son had taken in his mother-in-law, under similar circumstances. Much of this has changed in one generation. My mother, still healthy at 93, has been in a retirement home for 12 years. She preferred this option to living with me and my family, as did I; it helped to solve some of the problems of her loneliness and widowhood. My mother didn't want to be a burden on her children. She had opted out of living in the midst of her extended family, something virtually unheard of just one generation earlier.

In the past 75 years or so, industrial nations and private sector institutions have installed a variety of safety-net provisions which serve many of the functions that adult children used to perform, the most prominent of these being social security. Living with and being taken care of by one's grown children is no longer the only option open to aging parents. Yet many of us can remember a time before the prevalence of nursing homes, convalescent homes, and retirement communities.

The Big Bang

The Big Bang is the first-ever relaxation of the social imperative for people to work diligently at reproduction. As I pointed out earlier, the longevity timeline only started to arc upward worldwide in the latter half of the 19th century. Before that, population growth was almost steady over millennia. Small dips could be seen on the line, resulting from famines, epidemics, and plagues. But following these catastrophes, the line returned to its former level. Only very recently has the angle of longevity veered sharply upward. As a result, people in their middle and older years are able to see, in the course of their lives, how critical social changes have had an impact on every aspect of society.

In the short span of time between 1970 and 1990, for example, out-of-wedlock births zoomed upwards in industrial nations: in the U.K., from 8% to 28%; in the U.S., from 11% to 28%; and in Sweden, often in the forefront of new social arrangements, from about 18% to 47%. In the same span of time the marriage rate declined dramatically: In 1993 the marriage rate in the U.S. was 52.3 marriages per 1,000 unmarried women older than 15, a decline from 1946, when the marriage rate was 78 per thousand. The most spectacular changes regarding alternative families took place in the 1970s. Nevertheless, the United States census for 2000 has shown a large upswing in unmarried couples living together (71 percent since 1990) as well as a rise in the percentage of single mother households.

In my youth in the 1940s and '50s, bearing children out of wedlock was widely considered a social problem. Although the practice was, and continues to be, common among people living in poverty all over the world, it was addressed in the middle class as a problem needing remediation. All of this was questioned in the '60s and '70s — in fact, it was blown apart.

As with the physicist's Big Bang, the cultural Big Bang has ramifications in all directions. We are, as yet, so close in time to this unique demographic event that it is hard to understand it. For example, when marriage rates go up, as they did in the 1990s in some industrial countries (such as Denmark and Japan), it may appear to be a turning back to what some might regard as the good old days of the first half of the century. But if we stand farther back, it might also be a small blip on a line that is moving quite steadily away from the institution of marriage as it has been known for centuries.

This unique demographic event, which was building up to a boiling point and finally exploded in the 1960s, has deeply affected the way parents and their adult children relate in the new century. The reduction of the pressure to reproduce has resulted in bold and radical changes in the social fabric, such as:

- many women pursuing careers;
- men and women marrying in their mid-30s and older;
- a significant minority of women choosing to remain unmarried;
- couples choosing to be childless;
- large families (five or more children) becoming less common and less revered;
- unmarried women choosing to bear or adopt a child;
- homosexuality gradually becoming acceptable;
- sanctification of homosexual unions through marriage.

Just as objects moving through space make dents in the physical universe, each of these recent social changes makes a dent in the social universe. Parents are propelled into new and uncharted waters when their children choose to remain unmarried or when their daughters choose to pursue a career and then, at age 39, decide to bear and raise a child. Or when their son and his male partner undergo a marriage ceremony and decide to adopt two children. The parent can turn away, disapprove, or even disown such an offspring. But surely there has to be a better way, a way that will allow parents to appreciate the new options available to their children and the often difficult choices their children have made.

In sum, if the pressure is off having children, then it follows that the pressure is off getting married. The option of living in a social arrangement fundamentally different from the traditional idea of marriage becomes a reality. Young people may choose (and society is beginning to condone) any of the options or lifestyles listed above. The invoking of scripture or some other moral code to condemn, say, homosexuality, voluntary childlessness, or even women pursuing a career out of the home is doomed to fail. The power of the unique demographic event of the 20th century to change our behavior is too great. All of us, but especially the young, can only surge along on the crest of the wave, trying to keep our balance and not drown.

If young people have a new set of options to choose from, midlife parents have some choices to make as well. They may be discovering that they are not really old, certainly not in comparison to their own parents. They remember their grandparents who, at the age they are now, were seen as elderly (and who saw themselves as such). Parents in their 50s and 60s cannot help but be deeply influenced by the new sexual freedom (which is not really new to their children, who grew up with nothing else). Media of all sorts spell out acceptable (or close to acceptable) choices around sexual orientation, living with an unmarried partner, casual sex, and non-monogamy. While the midlife parent may choose to live in a conventional fashion, the world into which his child was born is now his world as well. Can parent and adult child speak the same language for the forty or more years that they may be simultaneously inhabiting the planet? Yes, but only if both parents work at understanding the world into which their adult children were born and of which they themselves are now a part.

To begin to do this, it is useful to zero in on some of the most striking social changes that have taken place in the last 40 years of the 20th century. First we need to identify the stumbling blocks that may prevent us from being comfortable with our adult children.

Women and Career

My friends, Bob and René, were in their mid-forties in the 1970s. Bob had a law degree and worked for the state bureaucracy in a middle-level post and took on private civil cases on the side, mostly for friends and neighbors. He made a comfortable living and the couple and their three children lived in an attractive older home. René was an uncomplaining homemaker, but when her last child left the house she wanted to take a part-time job selling in a gift shop. Her home and her life had become too empty. Bob didn't want his wife to work, and told her so: he felt it would reflect on his perceived ability to support his family. At first she complied: she identified with his "masculine" need. She also did not believe in equal pay for equal work or in women fighting for upper-echelon job slots.

"Men are the chief breadwinners," she told me. "Women go off to have babies. If women push for equal job opportunities, they're taking jobs away from men, who need them more."

But René became deeply unhappy without her family around her and Bob was forced to relent; he eventually allowed his wife to work! Not surprisingly, their two daughters are full-time working women, as is their daughter-in-law.

If you are a midlife parent you may remember when symphony orchestra players were all men (with the possible exception of the harpist), when elementary school teachers were all women (hard working and poorly paid), and the principal was likely to be a man. Vast areas of the world of work, both white and blue collar, were deemed inappropriate for women. House construction, plumbing, car repair, and contact sports such as boxing were deemed unladylike. Military service — actual combat — was not what women were all about. An operatic heroine was, of course, a woman. But a stage hand or a conductor was not.

My 24-year-old friend, Kathleen, is a boxer. She inhabits a world of woman's competitive boxing. She works as a personal trainer to pay the rent between matches. There is fairly big money in the field of woman's boxing, and Kathleen would not have to hold down another job if she won a few matches and rose to the top in her weight class. She is good at her sport and likes the challenge but isn't sure she will continue because sooner or later she might get her brains scrambled or her face disfigured. A college degree and a career in chiropractic have become her long-range goals.

Kathleen, born in 1976, never knew the-world-before-the-1960s in which woman's boxing was unthinkable and a career as a chiropractor was not at all common for women. Your daughter may not be a boxer but she may co-own a computer consulting business or be a landscape gardener or be pursuing a graduate degree in electrical engineering or be a wonderful jazz trumpeter. Your role is clear:

- to learn what your daughter's world is like,
- to help her learn what your world is like,
- to help her to learn what your world was like at her age.

Your adult child is operating in and emerging from a world substantially different from the world that nurtured you. You can better enjoy her world if you can focus on the larger world where all manner of careers for women are taken for granted. She will adore telling you about her work if you approach the subject as a learner (not as a teacher or busybody disguised as a learner). And, as the barriers break down, she will be fascinated by stories of your stay-at-home mom, her grandmother, and of gender discrimination — the all-male orchestra, for example, that she never really knew about.

Marrying Late

Midlife parents can remember, with great clarity, the pressure on young women to marry not too long after the age of 21. Single at 23 was still okay, at 26 it was beginning not to be. Single at 30 was a disaster. And, of course, the worst tragedy of all for a woman was to fail to marry at all.

Bev, one of my adult child respondents, did not live in a world where spinsterhood haunted families. At 26 she felt too young for marriage, although she thought about it and kept her eyes open. She pursued a career in law followed by graduate work in political science. She described her social life as a long series of relationships, including one that lasted six years which got stale and just petered out. As Bev put it, she and each of her partners began to think he could do better. Though her parents wished for her to marry, there was little pressure. They made it clear that they didn't want her to settle for just anyone, and Bev felt much the same way. Furthermore, many of her female peers were following a similar path.

When Bev found herself reaching an age when bearing children could present problems, she took stock and began a serious search for a mate. So serious was she that she took a leave of absence from her work in order to devote all her energies to finding a husband. She eventually did and, with some difficulty, got pregnant at 42.

Until a mere 45 years ago people were programmed to do their bit, to marry and to have a family. They started early, even in Western industrial nations — not long after adolescence. In 1958, a woman of my acquaintance, a professor's wife at a small, midwestern college, was elected "Woman of the Year" by a local service club. She was a quiet homemaker. Her "accomplishment" — the reason for her trophy — was that she had had five children.

Marrying at an older age guarantees smaller families. It is also associated with greater infertility, as women's eggs often become less viable with age; more adoption, including more mixed ethnic/racial adoptions (in U.S. families, one in nine children is now adopted); and the parenting of children and adolescents in one's 50s and 60s.

Your adult children have been born into a world in which these changes have been established. Take some time to ponder the ways in which your offspring are different from you because of these recent social developments.

Choosing to Remain Unmarried

The concept of bachelorhood has a long and quite respectable history. Men have been allowed to choose the unmarried state without losing caste. They could sow their wild oats without being shunned as undesirables. Their choice was simply an idiosyncratic one — reflected in the phrase "confirmed bachelor."

Women, on the other hand, had a lot to lose by failing to marry. The title of spinster was negative to the core. Elementary school teaching was one of the very few middle class, salaried occupations widely open to unmarried women up until the 1960s. The unmarried school teacher of the first half of the 20th century was expected to devote herself totally to her work, lead an exemplary moral life (i.e., no sex), and accept low pay and exhibit deep commitment (e.g., working overtime, doing extras) as normal for her station.

Working class single women were prey to unscrupulous men in and out of the workplace. Their reputations were constantly in danger of being compromised. Their job options were largely low-paying factory or clerical work or domestic service. Prostitution stood out as a profession where, if they were willing to give up on preserving their reputations, they could gain some protection and some income. Another alternative was becoming the non-working ward of a married sibling in exchange for doing some housework and minding the children. Whichever direction a single woman took, she was not greatly admired or appreciated by society. To women she might be considered a threat and to men, a temptation.

All of this has changed in the world into which your adult children were born. Your daughter now has a wide array of occupations to choose from accompanied by an equally long list of educational tracks. While concepts such as "ladylike" and "unseemly for a woman" are still around, their power to define a woman's options is decreasing with each passing year. Positions involving decision-making and leadership are becoming more and more available to women. Consequently, some women are questioning marriage. At the very least, it is becoming an option, not a necessity. And for many, their sex lives no longer need to be contained within a marriage relation.

We aren't hearing a whole lot about bachelors these days, either. Indeed, we are witnessing a striking shift in the connotations of the words "spinster" and "bachelor." Though the bachelor purportedly chose his state while the spinster did not, both roles are giving way to an ever increasing range of choices, the most prevalent being marriage-like, live-in relationships.

Choosing to be Childless

Up until the unique demographic event of the 20th century, the relaxing of the need for reproduction, married couples could not admit to choosing to remain childless.

For the first time, there were enough people on the planet to guard against serious population loss due to reproductive, medical, and natural catastrophes, at least for the foreseeable future. Only nuclear devastation, also a unique 20th century phenomenon, appeared to be the rogue element, the big unknown.

Midlife parents can remember when having children was not only normative, it was mandatory. Whether you liked children or not was irrelevant; you and your spouse were called upon to reproduce. If you tried and failed, you were off the hook. Possibly your friends and family felt sorry for you, but you risked disapproval if you openly rejoiced at your failure or admitted to a lifetime of birth control use. Opera divas, figure skating stars, and other prima donnas had an excuse — the unceasing demands of their professions — but just barely.

Openly choosing not to have children was one striking outgrowth of the transformative social revolution of the 1960s and 1970s. Before this period, women who did not want children sometimes suppressed the thought, taking part unwittingly in the social taboo. Few options were available to them. Birth control was imperfect, unreliable. One option was marrying at a later age.

Teri was a long-term and long-distance chum, an attractive, personable young woman who graduated from college in 1954. She took up modern dance in her teens and was able to make a career of it after graduation. She joined a newly formed troupe that performed on college campuses and supplemented her income from dancing with various salaried jobs. Teri felt enormous pressure from her parents to marry a man with prospects, and she internalized much of this pressure. But doctors and lawyers didn't cross her path very often, so she saved up her earnings and went on cruises for singles and spent extended weekends at singles oriented resort hotels. But something always went wrong. One way or another, every likely candidate fell through. When Teri passed the age of 30 her parents became alarmed. Her friends couldn't figure it out, since all pretty, nicely turned-out women with no obvious flaws were supposed to be able to find a man. Teri finally married at the unthinkable age of 40. Her husband, a house painter, was accepted by her parents as a last resort against the possibility that their daughter might be left a spinster.

The 1970s ushered in the era of reliable birth control as well as legalized abortion as a safety net for couples wanting to remain childless. Teri and her husband could count on not bearing a child until menopause took them into never-never land. In truth, Teri never told me she didn't want children. It is speculation on my part that marrying at 40 was a way for her to guard against getting pregnant. Teri was enmeshed in the taboo that made open discussion of the subject unacceptable. All we really need to know, however, is that marrying late did, effectively, reduce the chances of Teri having children. Teri's generation, whose values and lifestyles were forged before the 1960s, was unable to break the chains of the childlessness taboo, and often had to resort to devious methods such as late marriage.

Your adult children, by contrast, are likely to be perfectly comfortable with the decision not to have children of their own. The change, in a short span of years, has enormous ramifications. Among the implications are:

- Non-reproducing couples are just as acceptable, useful, and socially productive as reproducing ones.
- Because it relieves the pressure on population growth, some social critics now consider not reproducing a positive good.
- Not only is your childless daughter not an outcast, she may be appreciated and admired for her work as a first-class hair stylist, department store buyer, or travel agent. She doesn't have to become a prima ballerina to be relieved of the obligation to reproduce the race.

Unmarried Women Choosing to Have Children

Sheila was 28 years old in 1978 when she decided she wanted to have a baby. She was in graduate school, pursuing a doctorate in Russian and did Russian/English translating to pay the bills. Her father, a corporation executive, believed in his daughter and gave her generous sums of money whenever she needed a helping hand.

Sheila decided to look for a sperm donor, a man with no family history of disease, with good looks and intelligence, with apparently good genes. She found such a man and convinced him to stay with her to try to father her child. Neither one wanted him to play the father role, so their agreement was a happy one. Nine months later, Sheila gave birth to a healthy daughter and started down the difficult, pioneering road of freely-chosen, single parenthood.

Up to the 1950s, college women who were unfortunate enough to have an accident due to unprotected sex, mysteriously disappeared from campus, sometimes never to return. Their options, other than keeping the baby or putting it up for adoption, were a medically risky Mexican abortion, an illegal U.S. abortion (sometimes set up by a sympathetic family doctor), or a do-it-yourself, notoriously unsafe abortion.

If they chose to tell their parents, cover-up was the order of the day. If the woman decided to have the child, she might be sent to live with an out-of-town relative, if such could be found, for seven months or so. Or she might stay at a hotel specializing in housing women from respectable families who have gotten pregnant. The baby would then be put up for adoption and the young woman's life would revert to its normal pre-pregnancy state. From the parents' point of view, often shared by the young woman herself, she would still be able to make an appropriate marriage to a middle class man of substance. To this end, the woman was kept from view and the pregnancy covered up. Up until the post-'60s years, some variation of this scenario has been applied to marrying off daughters the world over. It is glorified in song and story and is part of the larger socio-economic tableau in which marriage is embedded.

The relaxation of the taboo against out-of-wedlock childbirth carried with it at least two other major value changes in Western industrial countries. First, it put to rest the concept, which is dying but is not yet dead in industrial countries, of virginity as a serious criterion for middle class marriageability. Second, it all but buried the phenomenon of the bastard, the disinherited child who suffers poverty, humiliation, and outcast status because his mother wasn't married to his father. Governmental safety-net provisions such as social security and welfare have reduced our dependence on inheritance. If universal health care and well-funded child care come into full flower in industrial and developing nations, we can expect that children from one-parent families will enjoy as secure a life as their two-parent cousins.

In sum, the adult child of midlife parents may choose to be a single parent without her status — or her child's status — being at risk. The great taboo against single parenthood is vivid in the minds of parents perhaps 55 or older. As with virginity (or lack of it) and accidental out-of-wedlock pregnancy, the taboo rests on the daughter's loss of opportunities for marriage to an appropriate mate. In the world of our adult children, however, marriage itself is being questioned and sometimes discarded. Accordingly, single parenthood carries less and less stigma; the taboo shrivels and dies.

As more and more single people, sons as well as daughters, choose to bear or adopt a child, the rest of us become increasingly aware of the physical and logistic difficulties of doing it alone. These difficulties, however, merge with the joys (minus the shame) of watching a little person grow. This is yet another glimpse of the new world that your adult son or daughter inhabits.

Homosexuality Becoming Acceptable

Midlife parents remember vividly the time, not so very long ago, when homosexuals could not serve in government or teach school. Coming out of the closet invited ridicule, harassment, and ostracism. Many parents, confronted with their offspring's homosexuality had to wrench themselves out of the conventional marriage-and-family box that they had grown up in or suffer a deep and painful break with their son or daughter.

Your adult child is living in a world where, more and more, homosexuality is a viable option. He may be in a gay relationship while also being a partner in a traditional marriage. He may have a homosexual partner or partners for only part of his life. He is living in a world where, with some exceptions including Bible belt backlashes, homosexuality is becoming a not-very-remarkable part of the landscape.

Societal acceptance of homosexual relationships — as well as other unconventional or non-childbearing arrangements — is inevitable. This acceptance will continue and grow as long as the pressure is off procreation. Your child has been influenced by these assumptions, and may very well be a practitioner of the new look in family arrangements. If she comes to visit you with a sporty girlfriend on her arm, if she has chosen a sperm donor for the baby she is hoping to bear, if she wants to sanctify the union by a marriage ceremony, be aware that she is not alone. Tremendous, unprecedented waves of social change are buoying her up and supporting her choices at every turn.

There is a reason why tolerance of homosexuality is growing apace. The proscription against homosexuality in the Western world has its origin in the Bible, in the injunction against Onan for spilling his seed on the ground. The Bible tells us to be fruitful and multiply, impossible to achieve by two partnered men and requiring new, unprecedented medical procedures for two partnered women. "Be fruitful and multiply" made sense up until the 20th century, even through World War II. But with the population explosion after the war, it became increasingly clear that neither developing nor industrial nations needed increased population. Homosexuals, then, were losing their negative status as the bad guys who weren't going to be fruitful. The unique demographic event of the 20th century had begun to release some of the pressure on gays and to welcome their manifold contributions to cultural richness (but not to population statistics.)

These are some of the more striking social changes that have taken place beginning with the 1960s that have influenced your adult child's thinking and behavior. These changes revolve around relationships and focus on marriage, family life, and sexual behavior. They influence a myriad of things — how one looks at monogamy, at child bearing, at homosexuality, and at the meaning of "adult," for example. Other movements of the 20th century that are not specifically related to these issues may have moved your adult child in dramatic directions, into places where you are unable to accompany him. The civil rights movement and the ecological movement come to mind. If your adult child has chained herself to a fence and been arrested in defense of redwoods; if she has picketed to advocate for ethnic diversity on her college campus; if she has talked about adopting a baby of mixed race parentage with a different ethnicity and hue than her own — your adult child's generation is showing. She will never be a carbon copy of you, nor should she be. Your job is to place her properly in the context of her times, her segment of the time line of history. You will love your daughter and your son more freely and fervently when you do.

Parenting is a challenge to all midlife parents. The remaining chapters of this book will describe the nature of this challenge and present steps towards possible solutions. They will encourage you to explore the beautiful terrain of adult/adult friendship with your grown children which you may never before have considered.

The challenges for parents:

- to recognize the many ways in which the legacy of the 1960s and 1970s has affected your adult children.
- to ponder the pivotal demographic event of that period — the relaxation of the need to reproduce.
- to place your son or daughter (and yourself) in their proper historical time frame.
- to learn what your adult child's world is like.
- to help your adult child to understand what your world is like, and what it was like at her age.
- to recognize that your adult child will never be a carbon copy of her parents.

2

SPEAKING FROM THE HEART

Communicating with Your Adult Children

"It is not wisdom to be only wise,
And on the inward vision close the eyes,
But it is wisdom to believe the heart."
— George Santayana

Parents in their fifties and sixties tend to communicate with their adult children much the same way that they did when their children were little. Their speech is peppered with "should" and "ought," as in, "You really ought to call your sister," or "Don't you think you should wear a heavier sweater?"

The relationship between middle-aged parents and their 25- or 30-year-old children has changed, but parents often fail to see that change. Even those that do see it, don't understand its implications and fail to draw up new, realistic guidelines for behavior in relation to their changed parental status.

In this chapter we will have a look at some of these new guidelines, which focus on communication, a critically important area of interaction between parents and children. Communication is the single most important tool for a peaceful and happy relationship between midlife parents and their adult children. If you talk but do not listen, your communication will be incomplete. If you listen but don't hear, it will also be faulty. If you ask a lot of questions you may discover a wall of resentment settling in. On the other hand, unimagined blessings may follow if you use sound communication strategies that grow out of love for your adult child and a realistic assessment of your new adult/adult status.

Improving Your Communication Techniques: the Basics

These techniques and strategies may be new to you when applied to you and your adult children, but, in truth, the practices described below are ancient — or ageless. Whether new to you as a midlife parent or old hat, re-think them as you read this section, and see how they can be applied in your family.

Speaking from the heart

What, exactly, does speaking from the heart mean? Sylvia Boorstein gives us her take on the Buddhist view of Right Speech. She feels that there is no substitute for truth-telling. It is a way of taking care of people. But, according to the Buddha, telling the truth is not enough. At the same time that we speak the truth, we should be helping the person we are speaking to.[1]

Of course, the heart — the actual physical heart — has nothing to do with speaking, except insofar as it keeps us alive. We use the heart as a metaphor for the spiritual core of our being where love and truth reside. One way to think about speaking from the heart is to focus on what it is not:

- It is not manipulative speech that is, at bottom, bent on twisting the other to our will.
- It is not cold, rigid, or business-like speech which fails to display feeling.
- It is not argumentative, bossy speech which does not allow the other to breathe.
- It is not speech in which one party expresses his feelings but neglects to listen to the other.
- It is not blurting out the first thing that comes into your head.

This last item is tricky. Why not blurt out whatever is on your mind? Isn't all of this a form of speaking from the heart? Well, perhaps. But if we ponder the Buddha's extra instruction, we see that caring for the person we are speaking to should not be divorced from truth telling. Speaking from the heart, then, incorporates understanding of and empathy for the other, qualities that also emanate from the heart.

Speaking from the heart is risky; your heart is (so to speak) rough around the edges. You will not always say well-modulated, warm and loving things. You may raise your voice, cry or laugh when you hear yourself speak thoughts you didn't know you had. Speaking from the heart opens the door to discovery, and discovery may be joyful or painful. But speaking from the heart helps you to reduce the need for secrets and to make it unnecessary to cover up those secrets with lies. You undoubtedly care a great deal about the quality of your relationship with your adult children. Accordingly, communicating with them is a good place to start practicing speaking from the heart.

While writing this chapter, I was mulling over a visit from my 32-year-old daughter, Betsy, who lives in another city. Feeling grateful for some wise advice about relationships and a wonderful, professional haircut which she had given me, I needed to thank her more fully. I called to tell her how she had filled two of my current needs absolutely perfectly: how I appreciate her wisdom (and would like to call on her — and it — again) and how much I loved my new, short haircut. I think I gave myself as much pleasure as I gave her.

Speaking from the heart does, on balance, give pleasure to the speaker. The pleasure and the healing it brings to both parties model a type of interaction for your adult child so that she will be more likely to speak to you from her heart — and it might even affect how she interacts with her grown children in the next generation.

Avoiding intellectualized speech

Intellectualized speech is speech that purports to be objective but is divorced from one's feelings: it avoids subjective response. Avoiding intellectualized speech does not mean you cannot analyze or engage your intellect in talking about, say, a book, a film, a current political issue. It means understanding and honoring your subjectivity. Subjectivity is a good thing; it is the heart and soul of your relationship with your adult child. There is no getting out of it, nor should you want to. Subjectivity is what makes you, as your child's parent, different from anyone else. It's unwise to deny it or to get too far away from it.

If your daughter has just purchased a new outfit and wants your opinion, you could say, "I like it a lot." Or you could say, "It's a good neutral color and goes with a lot of things you have. You could wear it for work or for dress-up occasions. Was it a good buy?" The second response, though not intended as negative, may nevertheless be experienced by the listener as negative. If you don't like it a lot, you could say, "Are you happy with it? Does it give you pleasure?" If your daughter insists on knowing your opinion of it, you must tell the truth, "No, I don't really like it, but if you're happy with it, that's the important thing."

The lesson here is to acknowledge the gap between your adult child's reality and your own. You may attend an art museum with your son and discover that you both love the French Impressionists with a passion. What a delight! But — alternative scenario — your son may want to look at the Alfred Hitchcock movie poster exhibit and be bored to death by the Impressionists. A speech by you about the importance of Manet et al will not work. While honoring your subjectivity — your likes and dislikes, in this instance — you must also honor his.

Intellectualized speech is used by all of us when we want to avoid raw emotion, when expressing our feelings seems too fraught with danger. With the section following you may be moved to discover a way to keep close to your feelings while minimizing this danger.

I-statements

I-statements are simple-to-understand expressions designed to defuse anger and resentment in the person to whom you are speaking. When using I-statements you express how you feel about something or someone, not how bad or good something or someone is. Learning to use I-statements with your adult children takes thought, preparation, and practice, as well as the un-learning of old habits. Consider the following examples of non-I-statements:

— What a jerk you are, hanging out with those no-good drug dealer friends of yours.

— You have some nerve cutting school for a whole week. How are you going to make something of yourself if you don't get a degree?

— How dare you speak to your father like that?

Making assertions and asking questions such as the above may help you to express your anger but will do nothing to defuse your adult child's anger or heal the breach between you.

Now consider these three statements re-configured as I-statements:

— I feel really uncomfortable seeing you with people who are involved with illegal drugs.

— I am unhappy about how your education is going. Could we talk about it?

— It makes me very sad when I hear this kind of talk.

It is a truism that you cannot be faulted for your feelings; your feelings just are what they are. Using I-statements gives your adult child less reason to want to get back at you or to escalate the fireworks.

I-statements also work when simmering resentment or anger is not at issue. Consider the following alternative opening gambits to a discussion of a book:

I really liked this book.

or

This is a very good book.

The first states only your personal impression. The second implies a judgment by unnamed others, by the book-reading community, by society, or by history. You are delivering an already-formed evaluation to the person to whom you are speaking. Your adult child has already heard a multitude of your opinions and attitudes and, especially, your judgments, over his entire lifetime. He may want a little breathing space in which to make his own, free of the weight of your experience. You can help him to make his own judgments by expressing your own through the personal pronoun. And, paradoxically, good intellectual debate is more likely to follow because parent and child are starting off from a more level playing field.

The only caveat here is that I-statements are somewhat different from "ordinary" speech. Many of us have grown up with name-calling and attacking, the mother's milk of many belligerent families. Some name calling is elaborate, multi-syllabic, or intellectually sugar-coated, as in: "You are so incredibly short-sighted; I just can't understand how you can be so anal-retentive." Or it can be short and sweet: "You jerk!"

The problem here is that we have trouble giving up our freedom to say things like the above, which work for us when the going gets rough. It cannot be said often enough, however, that they do not work for the relationship between midlife parents and their adult children.

The use of I-statements, therefore, must be learned and practiced. Two ways to do this are to attend mediation workshops and to role-play with a friend. A quick rule-of-thumb is to eliminate the pronoun "you" (as in, "You are a ...", "You never ...") as much as possible, substituting "I" (as in, "I feel sad that...", "I understand your feelings about...") wherever you can.

Improving Your Communication Techniques: Going Further

The basic communication strategies described above do not cover all expressive interaction with your adult child. Your child is going to respond to your I-statements spoken from the heart. What do you do now to keep the relationship healthy and to minimize tension? The next section offers tools for a wide range of interpersonal situations. After reading it through you may want to come back to certain parts of it again, focusing on the area or areas in which you feel you need a new start. Interrupting, for example, may be your particular bugaboo. Use the section called "Not Interrupting" as the basis for an on-going, self-paced workshop to help you with this crusty problem.

Learning to listen

Listening attentively is an essential ingredient in many disciplines, most notably counseling and psychotherapy. We listen to a friend who wants to cry on our shoulder, we listen to a three-year-old who is trying to tell us what happened, we listen to a teacher lecturing on calculus, Roman history, or Hebrew grammar. We listen to an answer when we ask someone for directions. But there are a great many situations in which we do not listen to another; or, if we seem to be listening, we do not hear. Listening to another implies that we care about what that person thinks or feels. This is especially apt in parent/adult child relations. Many parents, sad to say, go their entire lives as parents without wanting to hear what their adult child has to say because:

- they do not want to give equal weight to their child's opinions if they differ from their own,
- they do not want to validate many of their child's feelings.

Not wanting to hear what our child has to say emanates from fear. We may be afraid to give up final and total control. We molded our small children to our values, opinions, tastes, lifestyle, prescriptions and proscriptions. Now that child is grown, and we must face the fact that we are no longer molding her. But we often don't accept this gradual yet dramatic shift. We would like to retain a modicum of control over her behavior but we know we cannot control her feelings. We don't want to know that she can't stand Uncle Harry; we just want her to act decently towards him so as not to destroy family harmony and not to embarrass us.

We may not want to hear our adult child's views but we very definitely want her to hear ours. Carol C. Flax and Earl Ubell, authors of *Mother/Father/You*, admonish us: "If you [parents] want to be heard, lay down your weapons."[2] Further on they spell out an elaboration of this theme: "People will hear what you say only if they believe that you hear what they say."[3]

Jeff grew up in a home where his parents never once asked him, "What do you think?" or, "What do you feel about this?" They told him what they felt and thought, however, at great length. They never left an opening for another point of view. Jeff's older brother, Mike, grew up adopting the model of his parents; he was strong-willed, opinionated, and talkative. He felt heard in most situations. He passed this legacy along to his children. Jeff, however, was shy and withdrawn until he discovered that he loved to write. The written word became his outlet for self-expression, free of parental dominance. He published many books and helped others to find their voices.

We can help our adult children find their voices if we understand and face up to our fear. We can help them by training ourselves to routinely ask, "What do you think about X?" and "What do you feel about

Y?" It is surprising — perhaps we might even call it shocking — how seldom we hear people ask these questions in conversation.

Not interrupting

Learning not to interrupt another person's speech is exceedingly difficult if you have grown up in an interruption-prone family which is embedded in an interruption-prone culture.

The Glickman family, consisting of parents in their sixties, son and daughter in their thirties, and grandfather in his eighties, interrupted each other all the time as a matter of course. No one ever complained to another family member about being cut off. They talked loudly and fast, and the loudest and most tenacious speaker got the floor for a short while. Anyone who had anything to say would just butt in at any time. When James Glickman brought his fiancé, Elaine, to a family gathering for the first time, Elaine came away feeling frazzled and confused, not to mention unheard. She had tried to listen and respond to what people were saying but someone always jumped in before she had a chance to utter a word. She could never find an opening. The tension she felt, trying to find a way to talk to her future husband's family, obviated any pleasure she might have had at the gathering. She felt as though she were in a continual state of competition for the floor.

Learning to avoid interrupting one another can have a strong positive effect on midlife parent/adult child interaction. The balance of power is usually weighted in favor of the parent (although this tends to change as the parent becomes elderly). Allowing one's child to complete thoughts and finish sentences will level that power imbalance. It is sending the message to your offspring that his ideas are worth listening to. It is also implying that you don't know exactly what he is going to say before he says it. It may be something you can learn from.

Along with not interrupting per se, you might consider the following:

- If you leave breath spaces at the ends of long sentences, it invites the other to respond.

- If you say, "Excuse me for interrupting," tension is reduced, especially if you have been backsliding. For many, this will require conscious effort and practice. It simply doesn't come easily to a chronic interrupter.

- If you have a strong difference of opinion with something your child is saying, you might try waiting until she is completely finished and then say, "I have to say that I strongly disagree with you on that point." You will be much more likely to be listened to and heard than if you interrupt. You will have communicated the message that you are willing and able to listen — to tolerate — your child's entire argument, and that, in turn, becomes a model for your adult child's behavior toward you.

Even though interrupting other people's speech may be culturally sanctioned — may even be the norm — it is, nevertheless, anti-social behavior. The loudest, quickest, most articulate, and most aggressive individuals get to speak. The quiet ones often do not. But it doesn't follow that the former have more to say than the latter, have better ideas, stronger arguments, richer insights, greater wit, or more elegantly turned phrases. Jockeying for the floor can be an ongoing, competitive activity — for some, a dog-eat-dog activity — that the quiet among us have to adjust to. Parental sensitivity to this issue can go a long way towards repairing a relationship that is not what we would like it to be.

Avoiding invasive questions

It is very tempting to view the asking of questions as a positive or, at least, neutral activity. If we want to get to know our adult child more fully, what better way than to ask him questions about his activities? (See Chapter 6 for a more thorough examination of this topic.) But seemingly simple, straightforward questions such as, "How was your date last night?" or "Did you like the movie?" are often emotionally charged for the person being asked. Among the adult child's issues are:

- Does my parent have the right to assume that my life is an open book, that my movements are available for scrutiny, that I want to share them with her?
- Do I want her comments, opinions, guidance on every little thing I do?
- I want some things for myself. Why doesn't she realize that?
- She's assuming that we're buddies, peers. Are we, really?

People who are adults but not fully settled into the role may be sensitive not only to the authority imbalance between them and their parents but also the experience imbalance. They need to experience their world in their own time, in their own way. Sharing an experience with the parent may be perfectly fine when the young adult does not feel pushed and the sharing feels natural and comfortable to him. If you wish to maximize your friendship with your adult child, you will need to be patient and learn to sense when your adult child is open to and ready for sharing.

It is easier to understand and empathize with your adult child's response to the invasiveness of persistent questioning by thinking back on your own youth and young adulthood. Surely you can remember when parental questions, especially rapid fire questions, felt like parental control. To avoid feeling controlled, you avoided answering some of them. This may have made you appear rude or contentious some of the time, which wasn't quite what you intended.

Avoiding over-generalization

- You get tired easily.
- You never could take the summer heat.
- You always forget your keys.

Many of us get bogged down in hardened clichés around our adult children, presumably because we've known them for so long. We've repeated these generalizations forever, but have never taken time out for a reality check. Your adult child may have gotten over his childhood fear of dogs. Good for him. You can forget about dredging that up now.

Over-generalized statements refer to things that are not relevant to what a person is saying or doing right now. They are particularly destructive to the maintenance and repair of relationships when they include "never" and "always." A person doesn't want to be told that she never remembers to send a thank you note, especially as:

- the parent can't possibly know this,
- it is almost certainly not true,
- it is insulting not to be trusted to do the right thing,
- even if the statement were true, the midlife parent is out of the loop now, the adult child is on her own; if she makes a social gaffe, it's her gaffe, not her parents'.

Reality checking, from time to time, isn't a bad idea. If the subject of hiking comes up in conversation, you could ask, "Do you still get winded easily?" You will learn what you need to know and not get stuck in ancient history. (For a more complete discussion of getting to know your adult child, see Chapter 3.)

Cultivating a light touch

My 64-year-old friend, Seymour, told me the following joke: "I'm very depressed. I went to the doctor to get a prescription for Viagra. He told me it would be like putting a flagpole on a condemned building."

The humor of the joke, I thought later, lay in self-denigration. Making fun of ourselves goes a long way towards keeping relationships healthy. Many people can't do this because waves of insecurity about some aspect of themselves (their height or weight, for instance) make them want to avoid the subject altogether and to pump themselves up in some other area. Jokes allow us to make a pseudo-self-denigrating statement that doesn't come too close to our real area of sensitivity.

Jokes, however enjoyable, are hard for many people to remember and are not really what this section is about. Cultivating a light touch is. This might include:

- laughing at yourself for never (well, almost never) cleaning out the refrigerator. "Hey," you say, "I've got thousand-year-old bagels in there."

- admitting, without tearing your hair out, that you're lost on the road. "I think I was holding the map upside down," you say.

- letting it be known that you're terrified of cockroaches. "I'm going to get that #/?%!!*^$ if I have to call in the National Guard."

One of the difficulties that adult children reported in my interviews was their longing to be able to kid around with their parents or to fend them off with carefree remarks. But kidding around was next to impossible if they felt that their parents were too prone to judge and criticize and were too serious about "important issues." What a shame!

It is important to distinguish between a light touch and aggressive kidding. The basic rule here is this: Never make fun of your adult child. It sounds simple enough, but for many it goes against a lifelong personal style that includes making fun of others close to you as a way of bonding with them and strengthening the group.

Young males on urban street corners play some version of this, insulting each other (and each other's mothers, sisters, etc.) with ever more elaborate and foul-mouthed language. The challenge for each member of the group is to maintain his cool, not to appear to be hurt, to catch the verbal ball and to throw it right back. Presumably they are training themselves for life on the streets. Sociologist Erving Goffman put it this way: "Teasing, it often seems, is an informal initiation device employed by a team to train and test the capacity of its new members to 'take a joke,' that is, to sustain a friendly manner while perhaps not feeling it."[4] This may be so. But in adult life, in the context of partnering and child rearing, this trained insensitivity becomes counter-productive. Insulting your mate or your child as a toughening strategy works against traits of tenderness, patience, and understanding. And it is not understood by people who did not grow up with it.

In any case, "the Dozens," as this street game is sometimes called, is played among peers and seldom crosses generations. Making fun of your adult child to toughen him up will have a detrimental effect on your relationship, creating in him feelings of anger, competitive tension, and low self-esteem.

Refraining from giving unsolicited advice

Giving advice is often mistakenly thought to be an act of love. We care enough about our children to want to give them the best possible guidance so they can move through life as smoothly as possible. But, in truth, giving unsolicited advice is a substitute for love. This is because love requires, first and foremost, that we respect, honor, and promote our children's unique and special beauty. Smoothing their path for them by telling them what to do is, at best, condescension and, at worst, unwelcome invasiveness.

But it is an over-simplification to say that we should simply stop giving advice to our adult children. Susan Jonas and Marilyn Nissenson, in their thoughtful book, *Friends for Life: Enriching the Bond Between Mothers and Their Adult Daughters*, have this to say about advice giving:

> *At first we thought that the best way to respond to our daughters' transformation into adulthood was to back off, to stop giving advice, to stifle our impulses to tell them our points of view. But we soon became convinced that silence is not the answer. We've discovered that when our aim is not to affect our daughters' behavior but simply to say what we think is true, we tend to frame things differently and they are more likely to hear us out.[5]*

My mother-in-law, Esther, has become very close friends with my mother, Henrietta. Both are in their nineties. Esther was trying to explain her complicated eating problems due to bad teeth, including the need for soft vegetable dishes and nutritious soups. Henrietta couldn't resist trying to fix and advise. One day Esther, the more philosophical of the two, said, "Sometimes I feel it would be nice if you could just say 'That's too bad.'"

Saying "That's too bad," to your adult children is a fine place to start mending outworn or destructive communication habits. Try it, it's easy. Your children will hear it as concern and care and love. Most of the time you really don't have to say anything else. And your child will be emboldened to problem-solve, sensing that you have left him space to do so and knowing that you care. It is a mistake to feel that by saying "that's too bad" or even "uh-huh" you are doing nothing for your child. You are listening, you are probably hearing, you are validating, you are sympathizing. You are taking time to think about what your child has told you. You are understanding. You are trusting that your child will work it out. You are refraining from overwhelming him with your experience or knowledge. You are doing a great deal!

Refraining from talking too much

Some families constantly interrupt each other. Other families just love to talk. Sometimes they are the same families.

Talking — or, more broadly, language — is our uniquely human heritage. No other animal can produce the nuanced and precise communication of humans: in one sentence, for example, "John arrived home today," we are stating who did what, where, and when in four compact words. We can say so much about things that are not immediately present, things we anticipate, opinions, feelings, judgments, criticisms. By and large we love to talk. If we can't comfortably talk in one place, we'll try another. We choose our friends from among those with whom we enjoy relaxed conversation. We shun people who don't listen to us.

But talking a lot, expressing your every thought to those around you — especially to family members — can create serious relationship problems. With children, including adult children, it can have near-disastrous effects due to the power imbalance embedded in the relationship. Yet people who love to talk seldom want to give up the floor or relinquish their right to speak whenever they choose.

In the small-group context of family interaction, heavy-duty talking by one member means other members get to talk less than they might want to. And it is not easy for an adult child to ask her parent to stop talking. If the parent is exuberant, interesting, clever, or funny, others will applaud him as insightful or entertaining. If the adult child is left by the wayside in conversation, well, such is life. Or is it?

Speech — declarative or exhortatory — is not the only means of face-to-face communication. As a 17-year-old camp counselor I was unhappy to discover that I had to yell at my seven- and eight-year-old charges to get them to do the things the camp required, such as bed-making and clean-up. I felt like an army sergeant haranguing recruits. I admired a counselor in a bunk next to mine who never seemed to raise her voice and was calm and silent much of the time. Moreover, her campers performed all their chores and seemed to actually respect their counselor (not too common in the world of children's summer camps). "What does she have that I don't?" I asked myself. I didn't figure it out until many years later when, as a school teacher, I watched a few master teachers in action.

What I came to understand was that waiting for the floor and then speaking softly, deliberately, and succinctly, commands both respect and gratitude from others. And, after scoping out your style, people listen. With some modifications it has turned out to be effective for me with my peer relations as well, and in conversations with my adult children.

To find out if you are an over-talker when conversing with your adult children, you might ponder the following:

- Do you feel a parent has the right to hold forth for as long as he chooses?
- Do you feel you know more about most things than your adult children?
- Do you love to educate regardless of whether your son or daughter wants to be educated?
- Do you explain things more than once (on the grounds that your adult child may not have gotten it the first time around)?
- Do you love embellishing? giving detail after detail? exaggerating?
- Do you love being listened to, being in the limelight? Do you have real difficulty giving up the floor?

Finally, ask yourself if you are sometimes too cute, too clever, too insightful, too hilarious, too much of a wisdom monger. Is your son or daughter in awe of you and, if so, is this healthy for the relationship?

Your adult child may not be overly sensitive in the world at large. She may have good coping mechanisms and interpersonal skills on the job, with her partner, with her children, and with friends. But make no mistake: she is sensitive to you and to your behavior toward her. She wants you to give her equal time for self-expression. She doesn't want to be overwhelmed with words. She wants a chance to show her stuff in conversation. She wants her thoughts listened to, digested, considered.

Your adult child may not be aware that she is a little tense and anxious when in your presence if you are a chronic over-talker. She might never quite bring to consciousness this unpleasant sensation. Deep down she may feel you, as parent, have a right to talk as much as you want. She doesn't know how to say, "It's my turn, Dad," in a kindly way. And if you aren't willing to listen to her, you aren't likely to invite her to speak.

The only way to break the cycle is for you to become aware of your speaking habits, including over-talking, and to modify them so you can improve relations with your adult children. Here are a few suggestions:

- With your adult child's approval, tape record a conversation at the dinner table or in a car. You will learn a great deal about your speaking style as well as that of your children.

- The tape recording project may open up the subject of speaking styles to discussion. Take advantage of the opportunity. See if you can bring yourself to ask your child, "Do I talk too much?" Other issues besides over-talking may come out.

- Become aware of speaking styles in other families. You have heard and seen your neighbors, friends, and siblings interacting with their children over decades. But you may never have taken the time to listen closely, to assess what works well and what doesn't and to incorporate good communication traits of others into your own bag of tricks.

But, at bottom, the biggest barrier to modifying an over-talking trait is that talkers love to talk. It is a big part of their personality, their lifestyle, their way of moving through the world. Their talk helps them to connect with others, to give the inner self an outer presence. Talk is marvelously therapeutic for the talker. For those who talk too much, giving up the right to talk anywhere (excluding, perhaps, libraries and concerts) is resented and resisted.

Notwithstanding widespread love of talking, a good relationship between midlife parent and adult child requires a kind of "equal time" mechanism. A technique employed by people involved in an interpersonal discipline known as Re-evaluation Counseling is to use mechanical timers in conversations where equal time for each party is vital. If you are a chronic over-talker, developing a timer in your head will help restore balance to a one-sided relationship.

Many of the communication strategies described thus far are easy to describe but difficult to implement. For some of you they may require strong motivation and considerable practice. Learning new interaction skills means un-learning old ones. It also requires that you care a great deal about your child and about the relationship you have with him. In some families this is, sadly, not the case.

Diane's and Len's son, Ethan, was a drifter. He drifted from job to job — restaurant, ice-cream parlor, yard clean-up — and from school to school. Community colleges had their rules and standards, and, sooner or later, Ethan failed to meet them. When he wasn't working he would hang around the house a lot (more livable than the basement room in a friend's parents' home where he officially lived), play loud music, and raid the refrigerator. He would also discuss plans for the future with his parents who regarded these as grandiose and unrealistic and often told him so. He raised the subject of money fairly often, and let it be known that he could use some. At 29, Ethan hadn't accomplished much of anything — or that's how Diane and Len saw it. They didn't know how to treat him, what to do about him. He was in their lives, one way or another, that was clear, but did they want him there? Did they want a relationship with him at all? Did they think a pleasant or fulfilling relationship with their son was possible? Did they love him?

Diane and Len had trouble loving Ethan. He didn't give them any feedback. He didn't seem to care much about them. He didn't make them proud. He used their home as a hotel. They found themselves wishing he would leave. Learning good tools of communication with your adult children is only a worthwhile activity if you want to stay in relationship with them. An 80-year-old couple of my acquaintance got a court order against their 50-year-old, alcoholic son which denied him access to their house. They also changed all the outside door locks because the son was stealing valuable paintings and bric-a-brac and selling them to pay for his drinking habit. Communication was way down the list of things they felt they needed to do to survive. They had given up on their adult child.

Before you read further in this chapter you may want to ask yourself whether you really want a relationship with your adult child. Saying No to relationship means giving up on the possibility of closeness, equality, affection, sharing, and mutual aid, not to mention pleasure in and love for your child. Sometimes this is the way it has to be.

Do you love this person — your offspring — who is now a grownup of 24 or 31 or 37? Or has this adult child of yours gone in a direction so different from your own, so far away from anything you can relate to or feel good about that you prefer to direct your energies and affections towards other family members and friends? Is it possible that you cannot, will not, just plain do not love your adult child? Whatever the answer, it is important to know how you feel and to know how far you will go to keep connected. It is cleansing — and useful — to be square with yourself. You want to direct your good, loving, generous instincts towards people who will respond in kind, at least some of the time. You want and need some positive feedback. It requires sometimes painful effort to try to build a relationship with your adult child, especially if it comes to naught. You may have convinced yourself that you don't love your adult child, that she is old enough to take care of herself, that you don't any longer owe her anything, and that you wish to get on with your life.

But your adult child may have a different agenda. He may re-enter your life in a multitude of ways and at wholly irregular intervals. He may ask for money, ask for a roof over his head, invite you to his wedding, announce that he is to be a father. He may get seriously ill or have an accident. He may be in trouble with the law. He may be getting serious recognition for an accomplishment — an art work, for example. He may be homeless, mentally ill, suicidal. He may be working on you to be his first Fuller Brush customer. He may be writing a book about his family.

Whether you love him or not, you have carved out for yourself a place in his life and he, a place in yours. You are, most likely, going to be called upon to make some decisions regarding lodging, money, or other kinds of support and recognition. And the appearance of grandchildren may make you re-think relationship.

How do you feel about the relationship right now?

The following questions are intended to help you to focus on where you stand with your adult child right now, whether it is just as it should be or whether it can and should change.

- Do you avoid him?
- Does he avoid you?
- Do you feel tension in his presence?
- Does silence feel good or bad?
- Can you carry on a conversation easily?
- What do you talk about?
- Do you start with "What's new?" or "How are you?"
- Are there other, perhaps better ways to open up a conversation?

The above questions should start you thinking about practical realities of relationship. Take some time to look over this list and add other questions to it that are particularly cogent for you. Jot down responses. Check the issues or areas that you want to give some more thought to or to work on. Put a date on your notes and do the same exercise in a month.

The point here is to become aware of your interpersonal style — what you actually say and do or avoid saying and doing — in your child's presence. Becoming aware of your child's responses follows naturally from this. And knowing how you feel as you are interacting, whether relaxed or tense, warm-hearted or irritable, will help you to become receptive to healing and change.

Tension in relationships can have its roots in cultural taboos which inform our behavior but of which we are often not aware. There are several communication taboos which are embedded in our history and, consequently, in our lives. Deconstructing these taboos will put our own behavior in perspective.

Communication Taboos

The taboo against praising your child

In the movie of Pearl Buck's epic novel, *The Good Earth*, Wang Lung, the young protagonist, hears his wife cooing happily to their new-born baby and telling it how wonderful it is. The new father looks up to the heavens and, in a voice full of bluster and feigned anger, tells the Almighty not to listen to her, to recognize that this is only a plain, ordinary baby, a no-account baby. Then he chastises his wife for playing with fire, for tempting the gods.

Human sacrifice — and, in particular, infant sacrifice — may be the dawn-of-time precursor of the taboo against praising a child. We don't want to push our luck, the gods may turn against us, against the whole community. If we act as though our delicate and precious and utterly amazing offspring were nothing much, maybe God will give it health and long life. We have avoided the presumption that our child may be better, smarter, handsomer, or stronger than others in the community.

Another source of the taboo against praising your child is the notion that praise will go to her head: she will know she's smart, he will know he is good-looking. Both will become conceited and resented by the community as a result of this knowledge. Parents down-pedal their offsprings' talents and strengths in public, not wanting to show off too much (although grandparents are allowed some leeway vis-à-vis their grandchildren). But, more importantly, they often don't express praise and admiration for their children's talents and strengths in private, to their child's face, where over-pridefulness is not at issue.

Make no mistake, children of all ages never tire of hearing praise from their parents. In my interviews with adult children, a recurring theme was parents' failure to validate or even to recognize their children's accomplishments, including the ongoing stuff of their lives. (Learning more about your adult child's life will be discussed more fully in Chapter 3.)

The importance of praise — sometimes referred to as strokes — cannot be overstated. But there are problems in giving compliments. Flax and Ubell point out that "the trouble with these compliments is that they carry a hidden message."[6] The implied message from the parents is: "I know what's good for you, and I will tell you when you are doing well. If I withhold praise, therefore, you'll know you are doing something wrong." Furthermore, even young children detect insincerity. You don't want to be caught making flattering remarks to your adult child that you don't feel. What do you say to your son when he shows you an assemblage that he has created that you think is an example of the very worst type of modern art? How do you react when your 32-year-old daughter parades her latest outfit which is an ill-fitting, stretched, and wrinkled garment that looks to you as though it came out of the free box at the homeless shelter?

Below are some guidelines relating to sincerity that should help you to give praise more freely to your adult child:

- You don't have to like something that your son or daughter does in order to give her praise. Ask her to explain web site design, rain forest action networks, or Barbie doll collector's clubs. By merely showing interest and listening to her explanations you are providing acknowledgment and validation. Your daughter will hear it as though it were praise.

- Tell him "It's you!" You wouldn't have twelve antique clocks in your living and dining rooms all ticking and bonging away at once with no let-up, but to your son, the clock collector and restorer, this is nirvana. Enjoy his uniqueness, his enthusiasm, his knowledge, his craft. He doesn't need to be like you. He needs to be himself, and would like your acknowledgment for his individuality.

- Do yourself a favor and learn about current cultural icons, trends, and changes in perception. Recognize that we are all stuck in our pasts to some extent. If you were a teenager in the '40s or '50s you may have not have noticed when the Beatles, Bob Dylan, and the Grateful Dead arrived on the scene. But for someone born in 1954 or 1958 or 1963, these musicians were larger-than-life, more than entertainment, more than dance bands. You will need to know something about the significant cultural landmarks in your child's past. You may want to bone up on the loosening of sexual mores, including co-ed dormitories and cohabitation without marriage, as well as recreational drug use, rock/rap music, and even widespread computer literacy. All of these things, and more, have influenced your adult child's life. You will need to know about them if you are going to give him validation, recognition, and praise.

- Sincerity, after all, grows out of love. If you love your adult child you can appreciate her accomplishments even if they are widely divergent from things you consider valuable or beautiful.

Ellen's daughter, Grace, threw every spare dime into equipment for her darkroom. She worked as a waitress but photography was her passion. She took close-ups of plants, the results being more-or-less geometric designs. Ellen didn't know what to make of Grace's expensive, time-consuming hobby. The pictures seemed endlessly repetitive. Grace didn't enter competitions, have gallery showings or sell any pictures. She didn't even hang any on her walls. Ellen wanted to say, "This is not leading anywhere. Try something else," but she held her tongue. She loved her 30-year-old daughter and sensed Grace's pride in her craft. She heard herself saying, one day, "I admire you, Grace, for your devotion to this work. I couldn't do it." Grace beamed.

The Taboo against saying "I love you" to your adult child

Many parents now in their fifties and sixties grew up in homes where their parents never said "I love you" to them. This provocative finding emerged from an interview cohort of midlife parents too small to be statistically significant, but I think it is important nonetheless. Not a single interviewee remembered being told "I love you" by his or her parents even once. Why should this be so? What is it about saying, flat out, "I love you" to our children that has been shunned by many and may still constitute a taboo among middle-aged parents today?

"Do my parents love me?" is a deep and emotionally-charged question which most people would rather avoid. Either a Yes or a No answer to the question may be incomplete and unsatisfying. We can say, "Yes, of course they love me. They fed, housed, and clothed me.

They raised me to adulthood. They're my parents. Of course they love me." We may also say, "My insides tell me that my parents really never loved me. At bottom I feel unloved, unwanted, not okay. Maybe they tried, maybe they were convinced that they loved me very much. But something went wrong."

What is it about saying, flat out, "I love you" to our children that has been shunned by many and may still constitute a taboo among middle-aged parents today?

Provoked by my interview data, I wrestled with the following questions: To what extent is self-esteem influenced or buttressed by the utterance of "I love you" by the parents? Further, are there functional equivalents of the three little words — kissing, hugging, touching, and holding — that render the words merely one variant of expression of affection? Can a child feel deeply and securely loved and appreciated without ever hearing the words "I love you" from her parents?

Many of my adult child respondents could not remember hearing the phrase used in their home. Not only did their parents refrain from saying it to the children but they also didn't say it to each other. One respondent felt there was a distinct sexual connotation to the phrase "I love you" and that fathers, especially, refrain from saying it to their daughters.

Novels, movies, indeed most cultures (both high and low) invest "I love you" with strong erotic content. Of course, we can use the phrase to express close friendships or parent-child bond. Or we can use it lightly, frivolously — as some Hollywood stars are reputed to use the word "dahling." Nevertheless, the deep, romantic, feeling-tone of the phrase reinforces the taboo against its use by parents and adult children.

Saying "I love you" to one's sons reveals a different, though related taboo, a taboo against perceived threats to manliness. Sons, in our culture, are supposed to absorb the male values of strength, action orientation, and assertiveness, and not to place too much reliance on feeling. Over-sensitivity in males is discouraged. Saying "I love you" to boys as they are growing up may be seen as a "female" thing leading to softness, gentleness (heaven forbid), and the dreaded "sissy" epithet.

I suspect that many parents would like to tell their children openly that they love them, both in their childhood and in their adult years, but feel constrained from doing so. They may do a wide variety of things to try to convey the same message — giving gifts, services, advice, warm smiles — but the three little words themselves are avoided.

A person growing up in such a home may unconsciously imitate his parents when he has children, and perpetuate the taboo. Saying "I love you" is felt to be inappropriate or even wrong. Alternatively, he may make a conscious attempt to openly declare his love for his children regularly. I would like to believe that this can work, that people can break away from the legacy of this taboo without fear and without bad consequences for parent or child. To break out of the cycle of constraint, it may be useful to see how the taboo works.

When we say "I love you" to someone, anyone, we are giving them a great gift. If this gift were not routinely given to us, we probably wouldn't pass it along to others. Because we don't have to give it: it is, by definition, freely given. It is something bigger than a birthday present (a well-accepted ritual) or a holiday phone call. It is not a social nicety. It is not supported by custom (although it need not go against custom). It is, importantly, three little words, not ten or fifteen little words (I love you because you're such a nice, cute, little girl, etc.). Because there are only these three, unqualified words, we are saying, "Right here and right now, all of me is giving my love to all of you." So powerful and potent is the phrase in our culture that it is, sadly, sometimes avoided even in romantic love relationships, most frequently by men. Saying "I love you" involves devotion and commitment. It opens the door to intimacy. We may well ask, "Is it possible that many parents shy away from intimacy with their children?"

My interviews have shown that the parental taboo against saying "I love you" to one's young children carries over to adolescent and adult children. The adult child may then have great difficulty in saying "I love you" to her parents. One of the most strongly held feelings around this issue is embarrassment. There is something invasive, a kind of emotional nakedness, that clings to the phrase "I love you" that causes many adults to avoid it. It may also be that by saying "I love you" people feel themselves at risk of being rebuffed. The other party may not be able to reciprocate. That hurts a lot.

If fear of rebuff is really at the heart of this taboo, then the questions of who says the three little words first and, subsequently, who says them more often, become heartfelt issues. This is more apparent in romantic relationships, in which, typically, each party requires proofs of devotion or at least signs of affection in order to bring out declarations of love from the other. But however different the parent/adult child relationship is from the romantic one, the fear of rebuff, and it's offshoot, pride in not needing anyone's affection, are very much the same in both.

It is no fun to put oneself out to another, whether it be one's children, one's parents, or a casual acquaintance, and discover that they don't respond in kind. One of my respondents told me the following vignette: She and her father were sitting on the steps of the family's summer cabin in Vermont, watching a beautiful sunset, listening to the country sounds of insects and birds, enjoying the idyllic setting. Jean remembered this scene with pain and regret twenty years later, this scene where nothing happened — precisely because nothing happened. She wanted to put her arms around her father and say something along the lines of, "Gee, Dad, I love you." She imagined he felt a similar longing. But both of them let the moment pass.

I suspect that a combination of embarrassment and unwillingness to take that tiny risk of rebuff were what kept the interaction from flowering. It is certainly possible to feel warmth and togetherness in the silence of a sunset. But if a person wishes to say "I love you" and simply cannot say the words, a serious, culturally-based, interpersonal problem is being revealed.

The truth about loving is that it is infinitely replenishable and the more we give the more we have to give. But many people don't know this. I suspect many feel that if they give love too freely they will be depleted, and they must hold back from explicitly committing themselves to a gift of love by not saying "I love you."

Can we, then, make the leap and say that there is nothing that can equal the regular use of the phrase "I love you" with our children? I cannot, in all fairness, suggest that the total panoply of loving gestures shown by parents to their children does not send the complete message if it lacks frequent use of the spoken phrase. But I am haunted by the way in which the phrase seems to break down barriers to intimacy and break through to something profoundly healing.

You may want to wrestle with the "I love you" issue by answering the questions below. Get personal. Ask yourself how the taboo works, in what ways you partake of it and how you might be able to extricate yourself from it if you feel its constraints.

- Did your parents regularly say "I love you" to you?
- Do you say it to your adult children?
- If not, would it help your relationship if you were to do so?
- Do you feel constrained, embarrassed, or awkward at the thought of saying "I love you" to them?
- If yes, can you think why this might be?
- Do they say it to you?
- If so, does it make you feel good to hear it?

You might be surprised to discover that you would like to say "I love you" to them, and that you would be very pleased to hear your adult children say it to you, if they don't already do so. But yet another perplexing taboo keeps us from letting our children know this.

The taboo against asking for love

When a four- or five-year-old no longer asks a bunch of kids, "Can I play with you?" or, (even more risky), "Will you be my friend?" we know that an unshakable sense of me versus them is settling in. Before that age, a child can tolerate No as an answer to these questions, but once he perceives his separateness from all others — his individuality — he experiences rebuff in a new and powerful way. From that time on and throughout his life he makes veiled overtures of friendship to others, so that the blow of rejection, if it comes, is a glancing one and not head-on. We protect others, just as we protect ourselves, as sociologist Erving Goffman has pointed out,[7] from hearing these dreaded phrases:

— I don't like you.

— I don't love you.

— I don't want to be your friend.

Midlife parents and their adult children don't ask each other for love. Added to the taboo is the presumption that love between the two groups is already there. However, this presumption may not square with a person's inner reality.

Bernice, a 65-year-old widowed mother of three sons, wanted regular visits with her older son and his family living nearby. She felt she needed to bond with her two grandchildren and wanted to participate, somehow, in their family life. But when she was on the phone with her son, she was afraid to ask the simple question, "When will I see you?" When an afternoon visit with the family was coming to an end, she wanted in the worst way to ask, "when will I see you again?" but couldn't bring herself to do this. After thinking and talking this sore point through, she understood that she was asking for love and was afraid of rejection and rebuff. She was also uncomfortable about her own need for love, didn't want to admit it, and thought of it as shameful.

One of the ways we convince ourselves that our children love us is by expressive rituals: kisses and hugs upon greeting and parting are the most common. These rituals are designed to reassure us that all is well, that we are noticed, counted, appreciated, loved. Yet expressive rituals don't always get at our loneliness, our emptiness, or our feelings of loss when we no longer seem to be needed as parents. We struggle with the questions: How do I ask for the love I want and need without risking rejection? And how do I do this without making my children feel guilty?

Asking for love becomes easier when you consider the following:

- Your adult children would probably like to ask you for love and have cravings not too different from your own. But, having entered the world of adults, it may seem to them a childish, weak, or embarrassing thing to do. You can ask for love more easily if you focus on your adult child's emotional similarity to yourself and, in so doing, connect your inner need with her inner need.

- If you stay focused on your truth, there is less likelihood that your children will see you as carping and nagging, or feel that you are trying to induce guilt in them. You might say, "I'm feeling blue lately, I'm not sure why. I think I could use a little more attention than usual, do you know what I mean? I can't say exactly what I need — just to feel loved and protected, I guess." These are my words. Yours will be different. They will come from your heart.
- Your children will be happy to hear that there are specific things they may be able to do to help. It is when they can't help you — or when you won't let them — that guilt sets in.
- No shameful secret is quite as shameful as we think it is, and, in most cases, it does not have to be a secret at all. Needing love is a universal human need. Babies die for lack of it. You are understanding and respecting your humanity by expressing that need.

The fourth and final communication taboo is one that may encompass the other three. It is significant for all adult relationships, but analyzing and coming to grips with it can serve a particularly healing function for midlife parents and their adult children.

The taboo against talking about a relationship

In certain kinds of group therapy, an attempt is made to zero in on participants' reaction to other participants' behavior. People are encouraged to say things like, "I'm having trouble with the way you look sideways when you talk to me. It feels like you want to get out of the interaction." It is okay, in this controlled setting, to take off our masks, to be truthful about our feelings concerning the relationship. When this kind of communication is facilitated, we learn how our behavior fosters harmony or disharmony with others.

In everyday life, however, talking about relationship is shunned. It violates an unwritten rule of social interaction — that people be allowed to express themselves without their motives being analyzed and dissected to their faces. We might well ponder whether, in truth, talking about relationship is a useful thing for parents and adult children to do. As difficult as relationship talk can be — it can open up sore spots and reveal shameful secrets, both his and yours — it may be the best way to get on a sound footing with your son or daughter.

Karen's mother responded with "Why don't you..." to every personal issue Karen raised that could, even remotely, be considered a problem. Karen, age 36, stood it for years but never quite understood the source of her unpleasant feeling. Nor did she know why the "Why don't you..." response bugged her so much. She began to recognize that every time her mother responded this way she, Karen, would withdraw and stop telling her mother things about her life.

Karen devoted some serious time to thinking about and deconstructing this problem. After several thinking sessions she thought she had a handle on it. But she knew that expressing her analytical perceptiveness was not the way to achieve her goal of getting her mother to respond differently. She waited till her mother launched into her helpful hints routine, and then said, "You know, Mom, every time you say, 'Why don't you do this or why don't you do that,' I feel as if you see my life as one long series of problems waiting to be solved. Most of the time I just want you to say, 'Uh-huh,' or just listen. I know you care. I just don't need you to be always fixing things."

Karen had to understand herself — or at least be mindful of her feelings — in order to have this speech at the ready. She knew it was the relationship that needed to be addressed, a particular, repeated aspect of it. She dimly understood that she couldn't deal with the relationship as a whole — that it was too big, too unwieldy, and too vague. But by breaking it down, finding one imperfect aspect of it that bothered her, she could do what needed to be done. She had learned the importance of:

- working on bringing up and articulating her feelings,
- being concrete and specific,
- sticking to what she fel tabout what the other person did or said.

Karen's mother tried to shrug off her daughter's remarks at first by saying things like, "Oh, Karen, don't be ridiculous," and "I'm just being a mother. All mothers want to help their children."

But Karen persisted. She recognized her anger and knew that something her mother did was causing it. She knew that her relationship would improve if her mother would stop trying to fix things. She believed that the mother/daughter relationship was worth improving, maybe even saving. Her mother got it after a while, partly because Karen didn't gratuitously tear her mother down, partly because Karen believed in her cause and wouldn't quit.

The challenges for parents:

- to listen attentively to what your son or daughter has to say.
- to resist the temptation to interrupt.
- to leave space for your adult child to talk.
- to talk less.
- to use the pronoun "I", including "I feel..." or "I think..."
- to avoid making judgments and accusations, especially those which are expressed with the words "always" and "never."
- to praise your adult child at every opportunity.
- to tell your child you love him.
- to learn to ask for love without producing guilt.
- to figure out comfortable and unthreatening ways to talk about the relationship.
- to trust your subjectivity.
- to speak from your heart.

3

LEARNING ABOUT YOUR ADULT CHILD

Siblings, Friends, Work

"Always try to be a little kinder than is necessary." — James Barrie

PARENTS OFTEN DON'T SEE what is going on in their adult children's lives. As long as some basics are taken care of — they are coping, working, partnered — there is no need to look further. It may be seen as prying by the adult child. Furthermore, parents may not want to look too deeply for fear of seeing things they don't want to see. Yet if parents shy away from looking closely with understanding and compassion at their adult children's lives, an opportunity for a close, bonded, adult/adult relationship may be lost.

Your child's priorities may be markedly different from your own. Your 40-year-old daughter may adore her high tech job and show no inclination towards marriage and family. Your son or daughter's dating habits may be of the easy-come-easy-go variety. It was not like that in your day. But ignorance of your adult child's life — his values, priorities, beliefs, pastimes and activities — stands in the way of the rich friendship that you crave. Remember: you can love and enjoy your adult child even if he is very different from you.

My daughter Betsy came out as a lesbian at age 29. She didn't think of herself as a lesbian but rather as a person in love with Kathie. She had had a number of boyfriends, at least three of them of the live-in sort. She never made a serious move toward marriage and seemed to choose young men who were financially unstable and not inclined to settle down or even plan a future.

I worried about Betsy's financial insecurity, her unwillingness to pursue her education, her entry-level-wage restaurant work that went nowhere, her lack of a ladder to climb or of a goal.

Kathie came into Betsy's life in a city far from me and I didn't get the scoop till months later. Betsy thought of me (and her late father) as "cool". She wasn't expecting fireworks.

"Guess what, Mom. I have something really interesting to tell you. I have a girlfriend. Her name is Kathie. We're, y'know, in love. She's going to move in with me." That was it.

Betsy proceeded to describe her lover's qualities: "She's a personal trainer and a karate teacher. She's very good with money and cuts all those coupons out of the paper. She saved $88 last month on groceries. She makes stone sculpture. She's in college, but is taking it slowly. She's a very hard worker."

Betsy was right; I really was cool. I met Kathie, saw the two of them together, and kept waiting for the axe to fall — that is, I kept waiting for waves of disappointment, anger, frustration, and deprivation to wash over me. My daughter, my only daughter, was apparently not going to have the expected, the "normal" husband/wife and daddy/mommy lifestyle that had been so deeply imbued in me.

Weeks went by. The axe never fell. I felt no disappointment, only joy at Betsy's happiness. I spent some time in their apartment and witnessed all the same things that loving heterosexual couples must go through to establish viable couplehood. I saw the two women:

- getting used to each other's habits,
- sharing work,
- making little sacrifices,
- talking out differences,

- coping with jealousy,
- honoring and appreciating each other's strengths,
- being sensitive to each other's weaknesses,
- demonstrating their love and attachment over and over.

I couldn't understand how I got to this place of total acceptance. I remembered seeing TV documentaries and talk show episodes focusing on parents who were devastated by their children's homosexuality. Had I seen them that long ago? Probably in the mid-1980s, I thought. Something exciting had happened in the intervening years. I made my own reaction — of acceptance of my daughter's homosexuality — a subject for introspection and study. What did I learn?

I learned that I am — as we all are — a product of my time slot, my place in the flowing river of history. A mere twenty years ago it might have been different: I might have been disappointed but seriously conflicted about letting Betsy know of my disappointment. Forty years ago I might have embarked on a major, wrenching battle to get her to change direction.

As a product of my time slot, I find it richly rewarding to be a student of social change. This perspective has allowed me to perceive the transformations in my thinking that have come about as my culture has changed.

I have also learned that meanings, values, and context are all important. I reflected that Betsy didn't appear to love her boyfriends but has a fine, non-exploitative, love relation with Kathie. If one of her previous relationships had fulfilling, long-term possibilities, I might have mourned (briefly) the marriage and the son-in-law that might have been. But all "ifs" and "would bes" have disappeared in the face of my daughter's happiness, continuing growth, sensible decision-making, and affirmation of life.

My children can teach me things about the subculture they inhabit, about themselves, about myself. Casually, without any fanfare, I attended a summer evening barbecue at Betsy and Kathie's place. I met many of their thirtysomething friends — some gay, some not, some people of color, some not — eating, drinking, and, of all things, playing charades. To my great delight, I was not treated as the enemy, a spy from the world of grownups come to investigate the foibles of youth. What a revelation to discover that they were grownups, too! They accepted me — Betsy's mom, no big deal — and shared with me pieces of their lives. It was a multi-generational party that worked.

The motives for learning more about your adult child's life should not grow from a wish to exercise control. This principle is so important that it warrants examination.

The exercise of parental control takes many forms. One is financial: If the child does not meet with parental approval he may be disinherited, or his parents may withdraw current financial support. Another form of control is the withdrawal of love: parents may threaten to withdraw love if the adult child doesn't conform to parental wishes or values. Presumably an adult does not need his parents' love in the same all-encompassing way that a young child does. But withdrawal of parental love at any age is unpleasant at best, and can be a severe and traumatic blow if the now-grown child didn't feel that secure in his parents' love in the first place.

The motives for learning more about your adult child's life should not grow from a wish to exercise control.

If you are, say, a liberal Democrat and your adult child has become, to your amazement, a conservative Republican, your values are going to clash on many points: welfare, military spending, abortion, etc. Will you agree to disagree? Will you remain civil and respectful in family discussions? Will you love her in spite of her different point of view?

Still another form of parental control is promiscuous advice giving, which is discussed in different contexts in other chapters. Your role as a parent of a young child was to mold her gently in the direction of right thinking and right action. But is it still? Now that your child is an adult are your endless, unsolicited opinions on everything under the sun still wanted? Still needed? Your motive for wanting to get to know your adult child better should be solely to take pleasure in him, to enjoy him, and to love him more fully.

What are some of the things you can and arguably should learn about your adult children? Siblings, friends, and work come to mind because they cover so much of a person's life.

Siblings

Each of your adult children grew up embedded in a complex web of family life — your family of procreation. His siblings played an important role in his life and probably continue to do so. However, once your responsibility for mediating sibling disputes came to an end, you may not have given any thought to sibling rivalry extended into adulthood.

To differing degrees, sisters and brothers vie for their parents' attention and love. In families with two working parents, there may be precious little time for uninterrupted parent/child play, conversation, or touching. Attention deprivation can be real, not imaginary. In troubled or excessively busy families, children can perceive parental love as a finite quality: if sister gets more then I will get less. Whether this is a proven (or provable) axiom is irrelevant. The perception that parental love is finite — there is never quite enough to go around — always produces needy individuals who are ever on the lookout for ways to get more.

Your adult child may be looking for new ways to get you to notice, appreciate, respect, and love her while trying to sabotage similar behavior in her siblings. She may not do this, however, in ways that are readily recognizable. She may, for example, act as though she doesn't care a fig whether you attend her gallery opening or not. She may not even tell you about it. She may, in fact, be ashamed of herself for wanting your appreciation and approval so much. "Adults aren't supposed to care about such things," she may be thinking, "and, if they do, they haven't quite grown up yet."

If your children are secure in your love they will probably tell you about their accomplishments; they will expect that you will want to participate in celebrations of their success; they will not be devastated if you cannot attend. But this sense of security is often shaky.

Sibling rivalry doesn't just go away when youngsters become adults. It can take a wide range of forms from hatred and backbiting to avoidance to excessive formality and ritual gift exchanging. It can manifest itself in digs and jibes about the future inheritance. On the other hand, your children may have made a happy adjustment to this most persistent of family tensions; they may experience real love and affection for one another.

While sibling rivalry derives from competition for the parents' love, it also connects with the real life/real time issue of parental favoritism. There are any number of motives for parents favoring one child over another. Usually the favored child is one who, for whatever reason, causes the parent to feel less threatened and therefore to exhibit less tension or anxiety than the other children do. The favored child may fit the parents' ideal of beauty and intelligence more fully than the others, or he may seem to need the parent more; he appears to be less independent and therefore affords the parent a greater role in guidance and caregiving.

Favoritism may carry over into the child's adulthood. It is not considered "right" and so the parent often does not acknowledge it. If she does, she may attribute it to the difficult behavior of one child, thus transforming the basis for favoritism into a quality emanating from the child herself.

If you acknowledge the possibility that you have favored one child over another, you may be able to understand the behavior of your other adult children, which appears unfriendly, aloof, or rebellious. It may also help you to see your children's relationship to one another in a new light. Their rivalry from earliest times may never have healed, only gone underground. Your insight into it is the beginning of healing for both you and them. But there are difficulties and pitfalls along the way.

- You can be overwhelmed with the sense that sibling rivalry is your fault. If this feeling takes precedence over all others it can keep you wallowing in guilt and can blind you to positive programs for change.

- You can feel angry, disgusted, or otherwise disaffected due to constant carping and lack of goodwill between your children. You want it to end; you want your family to be happy. Yet, you feel you have no control over this.

- You can be confused about your role. Your kids are grown. It's up to them what they choose to do vis-a-vis their sisters and brothers. Where do you come into the picture? Or do you?

What can you do to minimize the effects of long-standing sibling rivalry? How can you maximize friendship among siblings and, in so doing, set the stage for greater friendship between you and your adult children?

- Avoid being judgmental. This first admonition may be the hardest. We judge our children (to their faces) because we want them to change. If we don't tell them what we think of their behavior, they may not know that we don't like it. Since we are the elders, the repositories of our society's values, our judgment is crucial to their development along socially acceptable lines.

  But wait a minute, whoa! We are talking here about adult children, not little ones. Do they continue to need our moral approval and judgment in order to satisfy societal requirements? At some point your judgmentalism will be counter-productive. Even if your adult children are behaving in ways you don't like, they will not hear you when you try to change them. They will only hear, "There he goes again," or "Is she ever going to stop?" or, "Nothing I do is ever right."

- Avoid comparisons. You may not ever have said, "Why can't you be more like your brother?" but you may say something more muted that nevertheless gets translated as an invidious comparison by your adult child. For example, you may comment on how his brother never forgets your birthday, or how his sister keeps her home so tidy. Become sensitive to your unacknowledged comparisons. It may be wiser and cleaner to confront your desires head on, e.g., "I feel bad when you forget my birthday," or "I really have trouble staying over in your house because of the messiness."

- Treat each child as if he were an only child. It's easier to do when your children are grown than when they are little. They are moving about in the world independently of you and of each other. Now may be the time to plan an event or trip: a shopping spree, attendance at a sporting event, a ski weekend, a vigorous hike, or an especially good restaurant meal with one of your children. (More about sharing in Chapter 6.) Decide beforehand whether you are prepared to pay for your adult child's portion. If you offer to pay, allow him to demur. Sharing the cost may help to level the power imbalance. In any case, being with your adult child for an extended period or for a short but out-of-the-routine period without other family members can be a real treat for both parent and child.

When I saw an ad in the paper for off-season flights to Paris at under $400 non-stop from the West Coast, my wanderlust was piqued. "Who can I go with," I wondered? Then it hit me. My daughter had never been to Europe. "What an opportunity for her, for me and for us," I thought. I knew I would have to offer to pay for her and I chewed on that bone for a while. It felt good; it felt right.

Betsy was thrilled and a little scared when I broached the subject the following day. She would have to miss some school and some work. But it was an opportunity very hard to turn down.

We spent two delicious weeks together — soaking up cathedrals and museums, eating at little crepêries, speaking fractured French, trudging up to third floor, walk-up bedrooms, sharing little things — hats, umbrellas — and doing small but vital things for each other. I helped her with the language and she massaged my feet at the end of each day. And we walked, walked, walked. It occurred to me that this was the very first time the two of us had been together, as adults, alone. We were mother and daughter but we were also two wide-eyed, enthusiastic and weary travelers together. There were many moments of unexpected fun, of unabashed people-watching. There were laughable glitches and false starts requiring two-headed problem solving (How do you actually get into the Louvre?) When we got lost, we got lost together. Betsy was quicker at negotiating the Paris Metro than I. We needed each other in all kinds of ways. But toward the end of the trip we both felt confident enough to separate for a morning here, an afternoon there. We were companions and helpmeets together. We were equals!

I probably won't invite each of my other two children to accompany me on a trip to Europe. They each have families of their own and serious time constraints. But they can each be my only child in ways that are custom designed for their own — and our mutual — needs.

- Don't avoid all-family events but recognize their pitfalls. This is really an extension of treating each child as an only child. All-family events (e.g., weddings, Thanksgiving, some birthdays) celebrate the fullness of family life. They incorporate all members, each of whom has his unique place in the family structure. They provide an opportunity for each family member to interact and catch up with all of the others.

  Don't be surprised, frustrated, or hurt, however, if your adult child declines to attend family functions. These functions celebrate the family but not the individual. Your adult child may have a residue of feeling, left over from her teens, that she is being shown off, that comparisons and evaluations will be made or that she is obliged to attend.

  In other times, in other places, the extended family or clan was the home base, geographically and psychologically, from which the individual radiated outward into the world. The comfort and protection one received from participation in family life was immeasurable. The restrictions on behavior and on some life options seemed a small price to pay for the protection, warmth and camaraderie of the family. But the 20th century saw the breakdown of the hold which the extended family had on individual members within it. People went their own way and did their own thing more than ever before. Your children grew up in this atmosphere of heightened individualism.

  What used to be felt as mandatory is now felt as optional. An extended family event such as Thanksgiving dinner could be deeply satisfying and meaningful to your son or daughter, but it could also be tedious, empty of meaning and boring. Let her decide if she wants to attend. Find out what her feelings are, if you like, but don't force the issue. Treat her as a grownup and she will fill the role of grownup with surprising maturity and grace.

- Consider family meetings in which each member gets to express himself on family issues close to his heart. These are markedly different from traditional family functions. They are structured in such a way that members can vent their frustrations and concerns without fear of ostracism. One family that came to my attention while I was conducting research for this book uses a "12-step" model. All members value self-exposure and honest expressions of vulnerability; these are considered vital to the success of the meetings. The older members of this family initiated the project and they continue to model self-revealing behavior for the younger members. In the context of the family meetings, everyone is equal.

Family meetings work best when specific ground rules are agreed to. A no-interrupting rule, an agreement to avoid name-calling, and a time limit for each statement or response are some examples. Some families may want to hold hands at the beginning or end of a talk session. Some may be buoyed up by a few thoughtful sentences at the start of each meeting by a rotating, designated family member.

Family meetings with agreed-upon ground rules in place go a long way to equalizing the power imbalances that all families have. This means that the older, more powerful, or more artic- ulate members — parents, grandparents, outspoken older child — have to be prepared to give up some of their authority in the interest of healthy family functioning. A wise parent can encourage this. It promotes family harmony based upon talk- ing about and coming to grips with real problems that someone is having in the here and now. It sets the stage for compromise and also for compassion. It avoids inauthentic let's-be-one-big-happy-family type thinking. Sibling rivalry, thought of as an underground river rarely if ever tapped but always there, may find its way to the surface in ways that are tolerable — and useful — for all parties.

Parents with only one child may never have given a thought to issues of sibling rivalry. However, if they plug into the right search engine, they may find out much from their adult children about the experience of being an only child. Some children long for a brother or sister and say so openly, but others may have complicated, ambiva- lent feelings. No one, not even a friend, may have ever asked them what it is like being an only child. You will find out soon enough if the question is appreciated. If you are also an only child, you may find that you have a lot to share.

Friends and Lifestyle

Your adult child is a unique individual formed by a melding of nature and nurture that is distinctly his own. You played a huge role in his life, but others besides you gently and subtly helped mold him into his present shape. There are things about him we inevitably do not — or cannot — know. Do we want to, and should we, be privy to our adult child's sex life, recreational drug use (if any), questionable or illegal business practices? And when does prying become a necessity? Where should a parent put the bar? When is intervention mandated?

In seeking answers, a parent must come face-to-face with the ethical question: Does a parent have a right to know whatever she deems important about her adult child? If the answer is yes then, under certain circumstances, she will learn relevant facts and do what she feels she must to remedy a bad situation. If the answer is no, she will accept his differentness or even his perceived weirdness with calmness and resignation, though perhaps a measure of sadness.

Parents place the bar — the point at which intervention is seen as necessary — at different levels. For some parents, intervention in, or even knowledge of, their child's activities ceases when he reaches his 20s. Everyone goes his separate way, with an occasional for-old-time's-sake phone call to punctuate the relationship void. Other parents do not expect a 42-year-old son or a 37-year-old daughter to have a truly separate life from their parents. Their biographies, and those of their spouses, partners, or children are open to continual scrutiny and evaluation by Mom and Dad.

Some adult children crave parental involvement; they can't get enough of it to suit them. They can even handle un-asked-for advice if only their parents show some on-going attention and concern. At the other extreme are children whose perception is that their parents are in-their-face at the first sign of trouble or pain. In the case of young children, neglect is the number one error a parent can make. In the case of adult children, it may be otherwise!

If you suspect you might be an in-your-face parent, take some time to ask yourself if the trouble or pain is life threatening. Carol, in the passenger seat of the family car with her 25-year-old daughter, Jennie, at the wheel, saw an out-of-control car coming directly at them. Jennie screamed but was otherwise unable to act. Carol grabbed the wheel and swerved just enough to avoid a collision by inches. Her clear judgment and quick moves saved lives.

Noreen, a mid-life parent, thought her son, Sam, a hard-working computer programmer, was looking wan and overworked. "You don't look very well," she ventured. "I think you need a vacation. You haven't had one in a long time, have you? Or maybe you could use a thorough medical check-up. I bet you haven't had a check-up in years. I'm a little worried about you."

Noreen's intervention style has many negatives:

- There is no emergency at hand.

- It is invasive; Noreen demands information that Sam may not have at his fingertips and may not want to search out.

- Noreen's worry is based upon a "wan" look that could have resulted from one late-to-bed and early-to-rise sleep cycle. She is filling in the unknowns with her own imagination.

- Noreen's approach is likely to raise Sam's hackles, as invasiveness so often does. (Raising the hackles of your adult child is generally a sign that you are doing something wrong.) He may dismiss his mother by saying, "Oh, I'm fine," which cuts off real communication and an exchange of genuine information about his condition. Noreen may have lost, for the time being, the opportunity to learn about her son.

If you really do not want to know something "bad" about your adult child, you probably should not ask her. On the other hand, you may be able to ask seemingly invasive questions in a non-invasive, non-threatening way — and actually get answers.

Noreen might have asked Sam, "How are things going at work?" (not "Are you working too hard?") or she might have asked, "Are the children enjoying school this year?" (not "It must be a strain on you trying to see that the children do their homework."). Or she might have asked, "How is the kitchen remodeling coming along?" (not "The kitchen remodeling must be exhausting.")

The first question is an unthreatening lead-in to the subject of work, a vast area of any person's life about which mid-life parents are sometimes surprisingly ignorant. (See the following section for more about work.) The first of the questions above regarding children is neutral and open-ended — which makes it more likely to elicit juicy anecdotes about the children. More importantly, your son or daughter will respond with a relatively uncensored, authentic account of both difficult, problem areas and of smooth-sailing successes.

The first of the home-remodeling questions above allows your son or daughter to talk about some of the stresses of home maintenance, sensing your interest but not your worry. Your adult children appreciate your interest, care, and concern but can do without your worry. Worry equals anxiety equals pain. When your adult children feel that you are worried about them, a guilt reaction is set up. They may feel that they are the cause of your pain. It is understandable that you want them to change, but change based upon guilt is not freely chosen and is interlaced with fear.

The key to learning about your child's life is, paradoxically, to be prepared to fail, not to get answers. If you act as though you deserve an answer (because you are the parent), you may get a backlash: your children may cease to give you answers; they may replace truths with untruths or evasions; and they may change the subject when they feel pushed or pressured. In sum, all personal input from our adult children must be freely given. If we push too hard, we lose.

As we saw in Chapter 2, sharing stories about your life — especially about your youth — with your adult children is a simple and productive way of leveling imbalances in power and experience. It can also be a way of getting your adult children to feel comfortable sharing their stories with you. It helps to be honest, to show vulnerabilities and weaknesses, and to joke about them. Besides helping to break down your adult child's resistance to sharing his life stories with you, you will be modeling useful traits for him. Furthermore, by putting some meat on the bones of your early schooling, dating or jobs, both you and your child can begin to see where his or her traits come from, the good ones as well as the bad.

One of life's greatest learning experiences is seeing ourselves in our oh-so-different children. (This is particularly revealing in the case of adopted children, where genetic factors play no role.) Your son, adopted at birth, is athletic, fast moving, shy, loves the outdoors, doesn't read books, is cautious and fastidious. You, his father, have two left feet, are an avid reader, gregarious, risk-taking, and messy. But after sharing stories (and thinking about them) you discover that you and he solve problems with the same combination of curiosity and logic, that you react to social injustice with the same outrage, that you both feel excessively pained when children and animals are in trouble.

Your child will love to hear your life stories and, inevitably, she will trust you more as she sees you as fallible. Remember, however, that a story or anecdote is not a sermon. Resist the temptation to say, or even imply, that your youth was better than hers, that your decisions were wiser, or that your challenges were greater. Your life was different, that is all.

Accepting the challenge to change some of your attitudes and behaviors will help to reduce whatever anger and resentment still clings to your adult child's responses. It will also go a long way to eliminating her need to prove herself to you — to prove, for instance, her competence, intelligence, independence, fearlessness. Ideally, she will more freely share with you some of her secrets, her fears, her life, as you share some of yours, all the while avoiding judgment and sermonizing.

When Aaron was a senior at a state college, his parents feared he wouldn't graduate. He had had a learning disability in elementary school, had barely made it through high school, and was gamely trying to pass his last semester at college. Part of his problem was that he was easily distracted and had difficulty focusing. He never admitted, however, that he had any problems, which frustrated his parents, Will and Anne. Yet, one day near the end of the school year, Aaron told his dad the following story:

"You know, Dad, yesterday when school let out, I was on my way home, planning to study for my big history final the next morning. As I was walking home, I saw this pick-up basketball game going on and I couldn't resist watching. After a while someone had to leave and they asked me if I wanted to play. I thought I'd just stay for 15 minutes, no harm in that, but I ended up playing with them for three hours. When I got home I was too tired to study for the final. I don't know why but sometimes I get distracted and get sucked into things when I know I should be somewhere else."

Will knew that the moment was magical. He detected the beginnings of tears welling up in his eyes. His desire to reiterate, yet again, the need for good study habits, gave way to the sweetness of hearing his son discover and feel free to share his own weakness. Will could have responded with a sarcastic statement like, "Aaron, I've known that for years." Instead, he merely said, "I hear you."

The first time your adult child shares with you a previously withheld episode from his life, you will very likely experience a transformative healing. Don't let the moment disappear; cherish it (small as it may seem), rejoice in it, seek to understand how to set the stage for more transformative self-revelation and sharing.

Once your child trusts you, there is no end to what she is capable of telling you. You will meet your adult child for the first time. She or he might share with you, for example:

- her fears around taking exams
- his shyness with girls as an adolescent
- her belief that she wasn't pretty enough
- his insecurity around money
- her difficulty imagining herself as a parent
- his deep disappointment at not getting accepted at a certain college

- her fears about competition in sports
- his sense of inadequacy over his height or his weight

These are all negatives (and secrets). But your adult child may also want to share with you things you already know about him, such as his love for jazz or soccer or gourmet cooking. There is nothing sweeter, especially if this hasn't occurred before.

Work

When I was in my late teens, I wanted to be a grownup; I wanted to work. Not baby-sitting (which I did occasionally) and not summer camp counseling (which I also did, for three summers running) but a real job, a nine-to-five job, a 40-hour-a-week job, even a sweaty, boring, repetitive, ill-paying job. I wanted to experience the adult world of work and the independence — the beginning of financial independence — that comes with that world. At the age of 18 I got a summer job in a candy store at 90¢ per hour. It was tiring, tedious, and exciting all at the same time. Receiving my first weekly paycheck of about $32 was a moment I'll never forget. It helped to know that I would be going back to college in the fall and would, in due time, have options other than an entry-level job.

In the course of my life I have worked at part-time, salaried jobs from which I couldn't wait to escape; entrepreneurial work which didn't feel like work at all, though it might have taken up 50 or 60 hours each week; writing, which also doesn't feel like work but which engages one in a wholly different way from being a shop owner or a wage earner; and freelance piecework, well-paying but insecure. Each of these occupational channels colored my life in massively different ways, each had different stresses, each rendered me almost a different person. Decisions to change work were big decisions with big consequences.

Most people have a varied work history and could relate colorful stories and cautionary tales about their occupational life. Work constitutes a big part of our biographies, and our adult children are no exception. A huge amount of each of our adult children's lives is spent training for work, thinking about work, and working. Yet it may never occur to us to ask them about it. If one of them has a job in the high tech industry, we may not have a clue as to how he spends his workday or what it means to him. We may spend our work days fixing broken pipes, making eyeglass lenses, selling women's clothing, or teaching violin. We've never thought about earning a living pressing buttons on a keyboard while gazing at a computer screen.

Or you may have a child who is a self-employed actor. She loves her work (when she can get some), collects unemployment much of the time, works in a restaurant occasionally. You, on the other hand, work as a school secretary or a bus driver, collecting a steady salary. What's it like, having on-again, off-again work? Have you ever asked her? Or have you thought — or said — something like, "You ought to get a real job." Conversely, you might be an opera singer, a top-notch tennis player, or a screenwriter while your son seems quite content as a meter reader for his city's traffic department.

Bob's parents knew that he was a professor at a state college but they hadn't a clue about how he actually spent his days, other than teaching classes. They knew nothing about faculty meetings, student conferences, administrative responsibilities, grading of papers, thesis advising, not to mention scholarly study, research, and publishing. Bob never thought to describe these activities — would they understand? would they care? — and they never thought to ask. A chance for intimate, loving, familial connection was lost.

There are things we might want to know about our adult child's work life, things that will help us to know him better and to forge a loving connection. We might want to know about:

- new occupational categories. What exactly does a website designer do?
- our adult child's attitude toward his job. Does he like it? Does he feel fulfilled? Would he rather be somewhere else?
- her feelings toward her earnings. Are they adequate? Are long hours and low pay wearing her down? Do her earnings make her feel like a valued contributor?

Your adult children would love you, their parents, to take an interest in their work. This extends to volunteer work and even to waiting for a call from their agent, who might have a small TV part lined up for them. How, exactly, can you do this?

- Ask questions. Everyone loves to talk about his areas of expertise. Find something you can latch onto that you find intriguing, unusual, funny. But beware: ask questions in the spirit of genuinely wanting to learn, not of trying to undermine your adult child's autonomy.

- If possible and appropriate, visit your adult child's place of work (although it might be wise to ask her opinion of this first). In all likelihood, your child will enjoy showing you off and his co-workers will be happy to see a new face. It's win/win all the way.

- Make mental connections with your own work life, past or present. You had to deal with a picky, uncompromising boss at your first office job. Some things don't change.

- Give praise freely
  — for dedication
  — for knowledge
  — for hard work
  — for talent and skill
  — for attention to detail
  — for a good way with people

- Talk about your work experiences but beware of the tendency to want to change the focus of attention to yourself rather than to your adult child.

- Beware of the tendency to want to fix things.

- Beware of the tendency to over-identify and to thereby go over the line from interest to interference with his job.

- If you can come to grips with your tendency to over-identify, ask yourself how strongly you want (or need) a better job or better line of work for your child. Do you imagine a job for her that is better paying, more socially acceptable, or that has more "class"? You and your adult child may have a very different sense of what constitutes class. Allow that difference to exist without trying to change it. And if you're not sure whether she wants a better job, ask her.

The challenges for parents:

- to refrain from asking your adult child questions about his life in order to gain control.
- to get to know her better so you can love her more deeply.
- to consider whether sibling rivalry may still be present in your family.
- to avoid being judgmental when you see your adult children quarreling.
- to avoid comparing one child with another.
- to treat each child as if he were an only child.
- to relinquish the right to know anything and everything about your child.
- to phrase your questions so that they are not threatening.
- to recognize that your adult child's communication about his personal life must be freely given.
- to cherish the moment when your adult child reveals some of her secrets to you, and to work at earning her trust so that she will do this again.
- to make an effort to learn about your child's work life without trying to manipulate, control, or fix it.
- to praise him for hard work, steadiness, dedication, or ability to tolerate adversity, and to seek out other traits and talents for which you can give praise.
- to accept the many ways your adult child is different from you.

4

SELF-DEVELOPMENT

*A Path to Friendship With
Your Adult Child*

> "Here are your waters and your water-
> ing place. Drink and be whole again
> beyond confusion."
>
> — Robert Frost

GOING INSIDE AND EXPLORING YOURSELF — your motivations, needs, areas of vulnerability — is a pursuit that is not for everyone. Many define themselves as "doers" — actors in the world. They plunge into job, hobbies, and social activities, impatient with introspection and self-analysis. This works unless or until something goes awry. The person who had "no problems" becomes aware that something dark and inscrutable is eating away at his composure, at his integrated, meaningful, problem-free life. He has never had to deal with sleeplessness, headaches, mental confusion, or difficulty with getting up in the morning. He has been avoiding his inner murmurings for so long that he doesn't have a clue where to begin to break the log jam that is keeping his soul confined. If the symptoms get bad enough he will get professional help and spend years trying to find his soul's truths.

But one can embark upon self-knowledge and self-cleansing at the first glimmerings of reflection — at 21 or 17, at 14 or even 12. Any age is the right age to begin to examine oneself — 50 or 58, 65 or 76.

Dedicated and unflinching self-reflection is a pathway to warm-hearted friendship with your adult children. It is not easy, especially if you have not lived this way before. In his book *Who Dies?* Stephen

71

Levine suggests that most of the answers and resolutions that the mind comes up with are just excuses not to go deeper.[1] But self-analysis is possible and it is worth the effort.

Saying "This is the way I am" is not equivalent to knowing yourself; it may be the first step, the opening gambit towards the lifework of self-analysis. If you admit to being afraid of flying (or of spiders or night driving or public speaking); if you become aware that you feel seriously embarrassed or anxious when your children are loud or shy or impolite; if you know you can't stand unwashed dishes in the kitchen sink or hairs in the bathroom sink, you have (as everyone does) many entry points to break into the secrets of your soul.

Dedicated and unflinching self-reflection is a pathway to warm-hearted friendship with your adult children.

You may want to ponder some of your characteristic responses to your son or daughter — responses such as sarcasm or aloofness or impatience. This sounds easy but it is not. You may regard such responses as appropriate to the occasion. It takes real effort to isolate them and see them as inappropriate — and as barriers to genuine feeling. We would like to think that our impatience with our adult child is due to her behavior — her slowness in making a job decision or her difficulty in following driving directions — but the impatience actually resides in us, not in her. If we can understand this truth, a multitude of parent/child conflicts are immediately short-circuited.

Consider emotional distance. Your parents may have modeled the trait of coolness for you, or the culture of your youth may have placed a value on undemonstrative behavior. But think on it a little more. Does showing affection cause you anxiety? Are you just a little afraid of rejection? Has your child actually rebuffed you when you tried to hug him? Is it possible that he feels you are rejecting him?

In this chapter I will focus on three mindsets — acceptance, forgiveness, and freedom — deconstructing some of the ways in which self-development in these areas opens up the pathways to unfettered love and friendship with your children. There are other categories of thought, feeling, and action that could command our attention. The list could also include:

- jealousy and competition,
- the need to control or dominate,
- perfectionism,
- avoidance/denial (including substance abuse),
- repeating familiar behaviors vs. breaking old molds.

If one of these is your particular nemesis, focus on it and make it your self-development project. Allow your intuition to guide you. If it helps, call your intuition God's instructions. More likely than not you will build a solid pathway to your adult child through your loving dissection of yourself.

I have chosen to dwell on acceptance, forgiveness, and freedom because they involve spiritual insight as well as psychological repair and improvement of interpersonal techniques. As with many transformative ways of seeing, the three overlap: When we accept we can forgive, and when we forgive we begin to feel free. Nevertheless, separating the three will allow us to look closely, to inspect the details, and to explore nuances in our own behavior.

Acceptance

Acceptance is a major theme of world religions. In modern life, however, acceptance is always tension-filled and problematic. The urge to fix, change, and improve pops up at every turn. Reinhold Neibuhr summed up this tension in his Serenity Prayer, written in 1934: "God, grant me the serenity to accept the things I cannot change, the courage to change the things I can, and wisdom to know the difference."[2] Not surprisingly, this elegant prayer has become the mantra of Alcoholics Anonymous, spoken collectively at the start of AA meetings. It could just as well be a prayer spoken at a marriage ceremony, at the birth of a child, or by a head-of-state during an inaugural address.

In exploring acceptance, the following Neibuhr-inspired questions come to mind. They are not questions with easy answers but rather thinking points that may stay with you for years, churning, provoking, and waiting for the right moment to find resolution:

- What personal qualities are you unable to change, and, therefore are forced to accept?
- What personal qualities are you unwilling to give up? What are the consequences of this?
- What traits or behaviors in your adult children are you unable to change? — unwilling to try to change?
- What is your moral position regarding the attempt to change another person, even (or especially) your own child?
- What is the relationship between self-acceptance and acceptance of your adult child?

Pondering acceptance can lead us into some rich, many-veined mines. Extracting the ore, however, is often difficult. We are obliged to accept the fact of our aging and the inevitability of our death — easy to say, hard to do. A major function of religion is to help us to explain, rehearse, and prepare for death. We are the only species that knows that death is inevitable; it comes with the package. It colors our lives in big and little ways. A healthy acceptance of aging and death allows us to cherish our time on earth and to work to improve and fine-tune those things that can be improved. Our relationship with our adult children may be one of those things.

We are also obliged to accept the facts of our individual histories. We cannot change, much as we might want to, our birthplace in a small town in the Ozarks or a railroad flat in New York City. We can change our attitudes to our past but not the facts of our past. If our parents were seriously overweight, never learned to read, or were wheelchair bound, if our younger brother was killed in action, if our sister got pregnant at 15 and had a baby — these chunks of our history have made their mark in our historical panorama, and these people have taken their place in our life's cast of characters.

In addition to the unchangeable facts of our histories are the often implacable "givens" of our bodies. For all practical purposes, we are unable to change genetically-based traits — our musical ear (or lack of it), for example. Coming to terms with physical infirmity, self-defined imperfection and what we might define as "stigma"[3] can involve a lifetime of hard work. A 6'2" woman or a 5'2" man in Anglo-American culture may stand out in a crowd as too tall or disappear in a crowd as too short. Neither one can significantly change his or her height. They were dealt a certain hand by their DNA, or, if you like, by God. Accepting that hand is a formidable goal towards which to work. Self-acceptance allows our lifework to be useful, integrated and fulfilling. It allows our unique beauty — yours and mine — to unfold freely.

There are many parts of ourselves that we may be able to look at not just with acceptance but with awe and wonder. Look at your hands, for example. These two exquisitely deft instruments of manipulation are whole and able. There are hundreds of things you do with them every day. Your opposable thumbs represent millions of years of mammalian/simian/human evolution. With them you can wrap a birthday present, give a friend a permanent, write a shopping list, practice the violin, hold a baseball bat, button your jacket, knot your tie, sand the turned legs of a country table, weave a rug or hammer a nail. Your life is immensely improved because you have opposable thumbs. Pay homage to them every once in a while; look at them in wonder. Then consider your feet.

After you have done this for your magnificently nuanced physical apparatus — even if parts of it are too small or too large or not working up to code — then consider your heart. Not the muscular machine that beats within your chest but the part of you that feels, empathizes, and loves. We call this "organ" the heart because it is quintessentially vital for spiritual life, just as the blood-pumping heart stands at the forefront of physical life and death. Consider the heart as it relates to acceptance — of ourselves and our loved ones and especially of our adult children.

By means of this heart we are able to stretch ourselves beyond basic animal satisfaction of immediate needs. We can see and hear and feel the needs of others with very different histories from our own. We have suffered in various ways, so we conclude that others — perhaps all others — have suffered as well. Author and critic G.K. Chesterton put it this way: "We are all in the same boat in a stormy sea, and we owe each other a terrible loyalty."[4] Can we feel compassion for our adult children's suffering instead of denying it or fighting it? Can we accept our adult children's suffering even when we, their parents, are partly responsible for it?

This last is a tall order. It suggests that we open a wound — or, perhaps, create a new wound — a wound that may throb and bleed. But the more profoundly you understand your children's suffering, the more you can accept them and love them.

The following three "if-then" hypotheses are another expression of this connection:

- If you can accept yourself as you are, then you will be able to accept your adult child the way she is.
- If you are able to accept your adult child the way he is, then you will be able to be a friend to him.
- If you are a friend to your adult child, then you will love her freely, openly, and without impediments and she, in turn, can love you much the same way.

Forgiveness

Forgiveness is radical. Both forgiving and asking for forgiveness go against deeply ingrained psychological and political truths. We fight against it. We reject its premises. We think we want to be — or at least, want to appear to be — blameless at all times. Admitting mistakes announces to the world that we are, after all, blameworthy. But forgiving others who have hurt us clears the playing field and introduces moral equity to the equation: By forgiving another we are willingly giving up claims to moral superiority. Judaism and Christianity both give forgiveness a central place in their teachings. Judaism devotes a major part of its devotional message during the period of the new year (Rosh Hashanah/Yom Kippur) to the difficult work of forgiveness. It recognizes that people have to wrench themselves out of old grooves to do this, and have to turn themselves in new directions. Only then can they begin to get in touch with this most spiritual of transformations.

Molly was a widowed homeowner in her mid-50s. Plumbing was one household skill she had never attempted. When the shower in her mother-in-law apartment failed to work, Molly called (from her very short list of carpenters and plumbers) her friend Peter, a man she had worked with on a city commission. Peter gave Molly an estimate, brought along his assistant, and performed what turned out to be a more complicated job than was first expected.

When Peter handed Molly a final bill that was $100 over the estimate, Molly looked at it, looked up at Peter, and tried to figure out what she should do. She began by asking for an explanation for the added cost. A small but bitter battle of words ensued. Molly then paid the original estimate price, after which Peter spilled out, "You never appreciate my work." Molly was flabbergasted, tried to protest, but realized it was useless. Peter had been holding this in for quite some time. She made a quick calculation and concluded that Peter cared more about being insufficiently appreciated than she cared about the $100. She started to write the $100 check when Peter simply walked off in a huff mumbling "Forget it," which left Molly feeling baffled, rejected, and upset.

After three weeks or so, Molly spied Peter at an adult ed class they were both attending. Molly knew what she wanted to do — she had been thinking about it a lot — but didn't know if she had the courage to do it. When Peter walked mutely by her during a class break, Molly put her hand lightly on his jacketed arm.

"Peter, I apologize for any pain or unhappiness I caused you. I didn't intend it. I'm sorry. I truly hope you will forgive me."

Peter smiled a little sheepishly and said, "I forgive you, Molly."

That was it, the end. Molly had given both herself and Peter a gift, a gift that had one important quality: it was total, unqualified. She could have said — and she had considered, many times, saying one of the following:

— We had a misunderstanding.

— We each made some blunders.

— Neither of us quite knew where the other was
      coming from.

— You probably were in a bad mood.

— You should have told me your feelings sooner.

But Molly understood that asking for forgiveness is best when it is without qualifications. Shakespeare voiced this thought eloquently in Portia's moving speech from "The Merchant of Venice":

The quality of mercy is not strained,

It droppeth as the gentle rain from heaven

Upon the place beneath. It is twice blest;

It blesseth him that gives and him that takes.

'Tis mightiest in the mightiest. It becomes

The thronéd monarch better than his crown.[5]

Once the other party understands that you are truly sorry for causing him pain, other details, explanations, and fine points may be discussed. But unqualified apology is so powerful an antidote to resentment and hostility that further explanations are often not needed.

It is easy to ask someone's forgiveness for routine or superficial mistakes. You know that your adult child, for example, will not blame you in any profound sense for forgetting to pick up his jacket at the cleaners or for not having the time to explain how to do e-mail, as you had promised. The wrenching difficulty comes when your adult child is clearly angry at you. She may cut off communication, refuse to listen to anything you say, or go into hiding. She may act out in a variety of ways, exhibiting rudeness, using bad language, pretending that you don't count, or even that you don't exist. Basic trust is lacking. Because of this, anything you do to break down the wall of animosity is doomed to fail. Anything except, perhaps, offering forgiveness. Offering forgiveness, like its counterpart, asking for forgiveness, is best when it is total and unqualified. One may acknowledge the guilt of the other; one forgives anyway.

Asking for forgiveness is a heartfelt, transformative, spiritual act. It is also a practical strategy for cleaning out unexamined grievances and, sometimes, festering wounds. It is a way of bringing sunshine and fresh air into a parent/adult child relationship, and of starting afresh on a new, wide pathway. In order to get to a place where you can forgive him you have to come to grips with:

- your own animosity toward your child,
- your own sense that the conflict between you is his fault, not yours,
- alternatively, your abiding sense that all his problematic qualities are, at bottom, your fault — and your pain in facing this.

A good place to begin is to accept on faith that your angry, sullen, or acting-out adult child is in pain. Some of that pain may have been caused by you. This is not the place or time for self-blame, however. Your less-than-perfect parenting came down to you through countless generations of imperfect parents, each working from faulty models and each trying to do her best. You — along with everyone else — are doing your best. Your adult child's pain can easily be inferred if you try to remember your own pain as a young adult. With a little effort you can remember how you wanted to achieve so you could show your parents that you could live up to their expectations; how you felt competitive with one or another of your parents and were never quite good enough; how they seemed always to love younger sister or older brother more than you; how they refused to even try to understand your differences in lifestyle. If you can remember (and re-live, for a short spell) the pain you experienced in relating to your parents, you can more readily accept your adult child's parent-related pain.

It is a short step from recognizing your child's pain to asking her for forgiveness. The words will come and they will be authentic — your words, no one else's. Best of all, your adult child will know that they are coming from a place of truth, even as she wonders what this new development is all about. Her inner ear will be making contact with your inner voice, a place beyond or before words.

Asking for forgiveness has a flip side which should not be neglected in your search for wholeness — namely, forgiving others. Have you forgiven your parents yet? Really forgiven them for any and all of the hurts they caused you? You may not be ready to do so — your confusion, anger, or inability to grow may be blocking the channels through which forgiveness travels. Never mind. You can start by focusing on someone who has hurt you — perhaps inadvertently, perhaps long ago — another relative, a teacher, a friend, or a co-worker. Practice mentally forgiving this person. First, tell them — in your thoughts — how they hurt you. Take as long as you like. Get it all out. Then think about the many ways this person is like you. Think about this person's pain if you can infer it from her behavior. Imagine — really imagine — that this person was trying her best. When you feel ready, tell her in your heart that you forgive her. Finally, ask yourself if your words reflect your feelings accurately. If not — if you still bear a grudge — don't give up. Try again.

When you have begun to feel comfortable with forgiveness and have been able to forgive at least one other problematic person in your life, it may be the right moment to think about ways you can forgive your adult child. Did he cause you shame and embarrassment by wetting his pants, sucking his thumb, or eating with his fingers way beyond toddlerhood? Did he cut school promiscuously and fail to graduate? Did she make a terrible marriage at the age of 18 only to get divorced two years later? Did she have an out-of-wedlock baby which you ended up taking care of while she worked? Did you give him some small business start-up money which he squandered? Did she borrow your new car without your permission, putting scratches and dents on the front fender?

Some of these, and the many similar parent/child scenarios and soap operas that accompany the growing-up process, may have bedeviled you. It may be time to mark them off the ledger, to clean the slate. Make this your jubilee year. Even though your adult child isn't expecting a statement of forgiveness from you he will hang on to every word you utter and consider your sentences coin of the realm. But remember:

- Forgiveness has to feel right, to be natural.
- Forgiveness has to come from the heart.
- Forgiveness is underlined by a touch, a hug, a smile.

By forgiving your adult child and asking him for forgiveness you have set the stage for your third and most difficult (but most rewarding) area of self-development — freedom.

Freedom

Of the three pathways to self-understanding — and to spiritual understanding — on which I have chosen to focus, freedom is the most wide ranging and the most illusive. Freedom from what? Freedom for what?

Does freedom imply irresponsibility? And what does freedom have to do with your relationship to your children? Of the many ways one could discuss freedom, I will focus on the following:

Love is best expressed from a place of freedom. A lack of freedom reduces the love and threatens to contaminate it.

Freedom allows us to find fulfillment in adult pursuits of our choosing. It allows us to fully be grownups. It helps us to grow out of the archaic parenting model of long ago when we were the chief caregivers of small, unfinished people. Freedom is knowing where your children end and you begin. There is a boundary line there; it is up to each of us to find it.

> *Love is best expressed from a place of freedom. A lack of freedom reduces the love and threatens to contaminate it.*

I was appalled when I found out that my daughter Betsy, in her mid-twenties, had $5,000 worth of credit card debt. Having never had a credit card myself up to that point, I wavered between moral denunciation ("How could you get caught in such a trap?") and fears for her psychological health. I urged her, over and over, to join Debtors Anonymous. I suggested she see a therapist (although the cost would fall to me). When her grandmother offered to pay the bill, I was cautiously relieved but shaky about the future. I even attended two DA meetings to hear what the world of debtors is like and to try to find some answers. Betsy was in the clutches of immediate gratification addiction, as I saw it, but I, in turn, was gripped by worry, shame, and fear. Her credit card debt reflected on me! What had I done to cause it? What was she rebelling against? Where did we go wrong? And how could a child of mine do something so dumb, so gross, with both her parents leading a lifestyle of blameless frugality?

None of these questions ever got answered. Instead, Betsy moved into her own apartment (working two jobs), survived, and eventually metamorphosed into a well-organized, focused, and financially independent person. Without my doing anything!

It is true that some crises are serious enough to cry out for intervention by parents or loving friends. Medical emergencies and suicidal depression come to mind. (See Chapter 5, "Crises", for more on this topic.) But for most of your adult child's less-than-perfect habits and pursuits, it is best to repeat the mantra, "It's her life, not mine." You might even come to believe it, in which case you will experience a freedom never before imagined. Two problems, however, might present stumbling blocks:

- Saying "It's her life" may seem unacceptably callous and uncaring to you, not the way loving parents are supposed to be. How can you calmly go about your life, enjoying yourself, even, when your child is pointed in the wrong direction or badly in need of help?

- Giving up worrying about your adult son or daughter may leave a void in your life. You may discover that you don't really want to be free of this worry.

The first stumbling block is a toughie — but not insurmountable. How can you enjoy your life when your child is not enjoying his? You can approach this dilemma by imagining the line that separates your life from your child's. On your side of the line, what goes on that will not/cannot be shared? Your sex life, surely, as well as your artistic/creative process, your deepest friendships, your thoughts. Your child has a similar line. He will not, or cannot, share with you his sexuality, his relationships, his thinking processes, his aches and pains, many of his minor (therefore not worth sharing) and major (therefore too full of conflict to talk about) daily life problems.

Finally, we each meet our Maker separately, in our own bodies, and experience life's journey on a different path. No two journeys are alike. You cannot, nor should you try to, take another human being with you on your path. Your path — your story — is yours alone, and it is sacred. We share landmarks from our path with others whom we care about, but the whole story is encrusted in our brains alone, and in all the cells of our bodies. We will never share the whole story. This may, unhappily, translate into loneliness for some, which leads us to number two above — not wanting to be free of worry for your adult child.

If you identify deeply with your child's needs and problems (described in some detail in Chapter 2), you may feel temporarily (and spuriously) needed and, therefore, not alone. Ultimately it staves off your own fear of death. It is also addictive. As with other addictions, you feel withdrawal if you can no longer give your child advice and help. If your child moves far away, is unendingly busy, marries someone who rejects your interventions, connects with a "bad crowd" — you will be out of the loop. You may still worry, but you can no longer help. Your parental concern goes nowhere, and fails to bring the relief from isolation that you crave. As with other addictions, your need increases with time, requiring ever greater displays of weakness, vulnerability, or confusion by your adult child to satisfy your habit.

There are many ways in which people may reject freedom, as Erich Fromm so eloquently described in his 1941 classic, *Escape From Freedom*.[6] We are concerned here with the simple but profound notion that not worrying about your adult child does not mean you do not love her. It cannot be said often enough that her life journey is different from yours — starting from the moment she was born. Eliminating the compulsive worrying over your adult child's development and, instead, focusing on your own journey will help you to love her from a place of freedom, and therefore to love her better.

Needing your child to fill a void in your life is a downward spiral that brings in its wake nothing but pain. One is never satisfied, and therefore one is never fulfilled. Freedom from this addictive obligation, however, can open the way to a less-burdened midlife and a more contented old age.

Where and how do you start becoming free? You can start by asking yourself, "What do I enjoy?" Or, stated in negative terms, "What do I no longer find meaningful, pleasurable, or fulfilling?" Here are some guidelines:

- Be ruthless. If at all possible, eliminate those things from your life which bring you no joy. When it is not possible, work on finding new angles and approaches that will lighten up elder care or the problems of an ailing spouse.
- Avoid martyrdom. In the everyday world that we all inhabit, no one benefits from it.

- Look upon midlife as an opportunity for new growth. This could be the deepening of an earlier interest that has been simmering on the back burner for years. Or it could be a totally new pursuit that comes to you in an inspired moment, such as learning a new language or taking up a musical instrument.
- Make your own enrichment, self-development, and happiness centerpieces in your life. Be your own greatest advocate.
- Remember: A major goal is to get you off the circular, unproductive and (often) self-destructive worry merry-go-round. It will give both you and your adult children breathing space and room to grow. It will reduce your neediness. As you advocate for yourself, it will dissolve pockets of guilt. You will be able to say, with conviction, "It's her life; and this one, this one over here is mine."

Freedom to pursue your goals and to allow your adult children to pursue theirs is a major accomplishment for you, for your child, and for the friendship between you. When you understand that this freedom from worry is worth pursuing you will have traveled a long way toward the finish line.

Loneliness

A discussion of self-development and inner work would be incomplete without touching on loneliness. Parents in midlife and beyond often find themselves alone through divorce or widowhood. Alternatively, one parent may be healthy and vigorous, the other infirm and in need of care. Some people suffer from loneliness and depression as they age and as fear of death wells up inside of them.

It does not necessarily follow that a midlife parent living alone will be lonely or depressed, or that a caregiving midlife parent will be isolated or resentful. But loneliness in some form is so all-pervasive a problem in Western society that it cries out to be addressed. Our relationship with our adult children is colored by our loneliness — the need for something or someone to fill a void at the vital center of our beings.

In Chapter 2, I approached the subject of loneliness by presenting the taboo against asking for love. A lonely parent may need expressions of love and caring but feel constraint about asking for attention from her children. She doesn't want to be a nag; she doesn't want to put pressure on these so-important people which might cause them to distance themselves from her. She wants to be a grownup, stand on her own two feet, enjoy her older years with courage and dignity, not be a crybaby. But the more she covers up her neediness the more it grows.

Working on issues of loneliness may have to take precedence over all other inner work. Clinical depression — loneliness carried to the point of illness and debilitation — destroys all of your own pleasure and truly does put a heavy burden on your adult children. In thinking about this type of self-analysis and inner work you may want to consider the following:

- It is important to differentiate between obsessive thought ("My children don't call me any more; they are just too busy to care a whole lot about me. I wish they would notice me.") and analytical thought ("Five years ago I wasn't feeling lonely, and now I am. What has intervened in that period to bring this on?") Obsessive thought is circular and repetitive; analytical thought is linear, and at its best can lead to a breakthrough in understanding.

- Beware of the time-honored truism, "Take up a hobby." Filling one's time with diverting activities is not a substitute for inner dialogue and self-checking. Spend some time discovering the right activities for you. You may be surprised to find that the old grooves no longer bring satisfaction and new grooves need to be carved out.

- Understand that sadness and loneliness are parts of life. Trying to eradicate loneliness without coming to terms with its source may result in pushing it farther underground.

- Recognize that it is unsound and unhealthy to curtail mourning. If your pet golden retriever is run over by a car, you may experience serious loss and emptiness and a longing for the companionship that only your beloved pet could fill.

- Recognize that all loneliness is a form of mourning over loss. The loss may be the remembered integration into a family or other group in which you were accepted, needed, loved, admired, or cherished. This group may no longer be functioning in your life, for all intents and purposes. This memory of past connection may be glossed and sentimentalized. You may have dropped from the tableau the memory of your competition with your mother-in-law or a never-resolved conflict with your younger sister, leaving only the memory of the contentment that comes with connection and integration.

• Pursue truth. Be passionately devoted to it. Avoid substitutes; avoid strands of thought that do not serve the pursuit of truth. Make self-understanding and self-healing your number one priority when confronting loneliness. Do not allow false gods such as addictive drugs, alcohol, sex, or acquisitiveness to distract you from your goal.

• Become sensitive to minuscule glimmers of light. Life's pleasures can come at any time and in any place. If something makes you feel good — watching kids on a schoolyard kick a soccer ball, for example, or hearing the first twittering of birds at the crack of dawn — make note of it and think of ways to expand the pleasure. Pleasures of the senses and of the intellect are gifts which, for most of us, are there for the taking. Pleasures can be harvested each day, each hour. Each pleasure that we allow into our consciousness relieves a pang of loneliness.

• A glimmer of light may also be an insight. Be sensitive to the still, small voice in which insights often unveil themselves. Find a way to get away from everyday tasks long enough to trap the insight for later exploration. Write it down or tell it to a friend: don't let it get away.

Your adult children may or may not be able to fill the void of your loneliness. Most likely they will not. Rehashing fantasies of perfect, loving, considerate, and caring adult children, with you an integral part of ongoing, rich, seamless family life is doomed to backfire and to cause you pain. There is no substitute for building a life for yourself that will withstand your adult children's inadvertent neglect, annoying habits, unfamiliar lifestyle, or, in some cases, their unfriendly, resentful, or exploitative behavior. You are blessed if your children like you and doubly blessed if they let you know it.

The challenges for parents:

- to honor and cherish your gloriously complex body, soul, and intellect.
- to remember and honor your suffering.
- to recognize and honor the suffering of your adult children.
- to understand that self-acceptance leads to acceptance of your adult children.
- to forgive someone who has hurt you.
- when you feel comfortable with the idea, to forgive your adult children.
- to ask for forgiveness from someone you have hurt.
- to ask for forgiveness from your adult children.
- to find ways to share your loneliness with your adult children without creating guilt.
- to make curbing loneliness a number one priority.

5

CRISES

When Something Goes Wrong in Your Adult Child's Life

There are moments when everything goes
well; don't be frightened, it won't last.
— Jules Renard

ALL PARENTS HAVE PRECONCEIVED NOTIONS of how their children should live. As with the rest of humanity, parents have positions on almost everything and are often bogged down in prejudices which harden into quick answers and brittle clichés. If your son becomes a drug dealer and, let us say, a rock band drummer (not a solid, middle-class profession), you may suffer disappointment and/or fear for your child's health and safety. But if his band succeeds and he becomes rich and famous, the disappointment and fear come up against that other major value — desire for your child's success. As a parent, you face a formidable challenge: how to become comfortable with your adult child's lifestyle.

Crises may occur in your adult child's life around almost anything: health, an accident, inability to get or hold a job, a relationship. Besides disappointment and fear for your child's health or safety, there are other fears and difficulties that you face as a parent: You may fear that your child will change radically, will nevermore be the "child" you used to know. You may be haunted by the thought that your child will go away and never come back. You may have great difficulty seeing your child experiencing pain, yet you may find that your offer of help is rejected or makes matter worse. And what you have defined as pain may not be felt as pain by your son or daughter.

But crises — sometimes very serious ones — do occur. It is not that easy for a parent to shrug off crises, to say, "Whatever will be will be." And the line between "crisis" and "different lifestyle" may be blurred. In this chapter, I take a magnifying glass to the concept of crisis as it relates to your adult child. Continuing the theme of interference and intervention begun in Chapter 3, I examine what constitutes a crisis in your adult child's life and what you can and should do about it.

Your Definition of Crisis

Chronic versus acute problems

A life-threatening crisis demands action. Rule #1 is always to grab the wheel in the face of an oncoming car. If the action is accompanied by screaming or crying, so be it. All niceties are tabled in the face of immediate, critical needs of our loved ones and ourselves. There is no time for moderated, controlled, or nuanced behavior. Our adrenaline is flowing, helping us to move fast, to lift, push, or pull beyond our usual capacities. Our bodies know there is a crisis and help us to deal with it. If we scream, "Watch out!" it is probably the appropriate thing to do. But many seemingly critical situations are of a different order.

Angela, 69, lived in a small apartment complex which she owned. She rented one apartment to her unmarried, working daughter, Martha, 34, who had a 10-month-old baby. Martha nursed her baby daughter, which necessitated getting up twice each night. Angela thought the nursing was tiring Martha to a point that would compromise her health. She also thought Martha would have to quit work and not be able to pay the rent, a part of Angela's livelihood. Angela expressed her fears over and over to her daughter, who responded with pique and sullenness.

But Martha was also very articulate. "Don't you think its time you left me alone, Mom? I like to nurse; it's good for the baby and it's good for me. I've heard your arguments many times. If you keep saying these things I just get angry and don't listen anymore. All you have to do is tell me once about the rent, not 20 times. I'll pay it or else I'll leave."

Angela's communications were based on her assumption: "If she doesn't listen to me the first time maybe I need to repeat it louder and stronger." Martha's response is based on her assumption: "If she doesn't shut up after giving me her opinion, she doesn't trust me to be smart enough to get it the first time." The relationship is set up for bad blood, chronic misunderstanding, and miscommunication which, sad to say, can last a lifetime.

Both Angela and Martha have to get un-stuck from their positions. A reliable and useful way to do this is for each party to repeat what the other has just said. If Angela can state Martha's position (in Angela's own words) and Martha can do likewise, they will inevitably begin to act the part of the other and feel the other's feelings. This is a powerful tool for reconciliation. Angela and Martha will very likely discover that each other's position is not so untenable and is based on all-too-human motivations. Stating the other party's position can be built into all parent/adult child interpersonal conflicts. It needs to be said, however, that you, the parent, should make the first move. Author and psychotherapist Eric Maisel, has said this eloquently:

> *What there is to work with is the love that already exists, the hope in each family member's heart for something better, and the innate power of individual people to try harder, beginning with you. You can't ask your husband or wife [or] son or daughter to do a better job of communicating if you aren't striving to be an honest, effective listener and speaker. The ball is in your court.[1]*

The following is a list of chronic problems that your son or daughter may be embroiled in from time to time. Typically, these are problems that may be thorny but are not life-threatening. The list is not inclusive: mull it over, think about it, and add to it. Once you understand the distinction between chronic and acute, you can develop a customized list that includes special issues and problems particularly relevant to your family. These are ongoing problems that require little if any intervention from you.

Chronic Problems

- Money woes. Your adult child is earning enough to be financially secure but is always in debt; he might be working 40 hours per week but can't make ends meet; he doesn't work at a job for more than a year, then, typically, goes on unemployment; he gambles, loans money to friends, buys expensive gifts for others, or is a spendthrift himself.

- Marital difficulties. Your adult child and her spouse are constantly carping in your presence; you sense that their relationship is not going smoothly; your adult child tells you more than you want to know about her partner's bad traits; you don't know whether the marriage is worth saving.

- Problems with your children's children. One or more of them is doing poorly in school; one is very shy, another, very aggressive; one, a toddler, cries a lot or wets his bed at night; one has physical at-risk problems such as allergies or ear infections.

- Chronic stress, low level depression. Your adult child complains often about having too much to do and not enough time in which to do it; you learn that she is taking tranquilizers or antidepressants; she overeats or under-eats; she has bouts of insomnia; she yells at her children at the drop of a hat.

- Substance use/abuse. Your son can't or won't give up smoking; your daughter drinks a few cocktails every evening before dinner and occasionally more drinks after dinner; your children smoke marijuana at parties and have tried cocaine, although you don't know how often.

- Driving. Your adult child drives five to ten miles per hour over the speed limit; he has been given a few traffic tickets and has been involved in a few minor accidents; he sometimes asks to borrow your car; you are scared both for him and for yourself when you are in a car that he is driving.

If we look at critical problems and situations as either chronic or acute, we will see that Martha's were chronic. Mother and daughter could have (and probably should have) discussed these issues earlier. Now Angela needs to back off trying to change her daughter.

The line separating chronic from acute problems isn't always clear cut. Parents differ about where to

> *When was the last time your adult child really listened to you when you tried to give him driving or debt management tips?*

place the line separating, for example, substance use from substance abuse. If a parent has indulged in recreational drugs, she will probably take a relaxed view of her adult child's recreational drug use. If she has a strong anti-drug bias, she may look upon her child's drug use with fear or horror, and define it as critical and therefore in need of immediate intervention.

To argue that parents should not intervene in chronic, problematic life issues of their adult children would be an oversimplification. The purpose of separating the chronic from the acute, however, is to start you thinking about ongoing stress vs. suicidal depression, debt problems vs. eviction for non-payment of rent, bad driving habits vs. a car accident, marital quarreling vs. physical abuse. Ideally, a parent would like to help her adult child before she is suicidal, evicted, has a car accident, or is beaten by her spouse. It is sad, indeed, to have to wait until something dire happens before offering succor — along with time, energy and money. But ask yourself this: When was the last time your adult child really listened to you when you tried to give him driving or debt management tips?

When your adult child's problems are chronic rather than acute, your possibilities for successful intervention are seriously limited.

It is also useful to be aware of subjective factors that make us particularly fearful concerning some aspect of our adult child's life. The mechanism of projection may be at the root of many such fears. Mariana Caplan, author of *When Sons and Daughters Choose Alternative Lifestyles,* defines projection this way:

> *Psychologically speaking, projection is the process by which we displace the origin of certain thoughts and emotions, placing them onto someone or something outside of ourselves.*[2]

Caplan goes on to give a cogent example of projection:

a parent who learned, as a child, that his was the only true religion and that failure to practice that religion meant condemnation to hell, may have also learned to suppress all of his curiosity about who or what God is, and about the belief systems of other religions. When his adult-child chooses to live at a Buddhist meditation center, or a Quaker farm, this parent's ancient fears are stirred. Without even remembering his own original curiosity, or without questioning the assumptions upon which his fear is based, he projects this fear onto his adult-child and becomes terrified for her, convinced that she will not be "saved" or that she will be sent to hell. The fear that he feels originates from his own reality, and does not actually take into account the actual circumstances of his adult-child's life.[3]

Projection aside, acute problems can and do exist. As with the foregoing list, the list below is also incomplete. It is a sample of acute problems that may have been visited upon your adult children or on their children. These problems are characterized by immediacy, intensity, and pain. They cannot go on and on; something must be done right away. They are sometimes life-threatening and call for immediate intervention.

Acute problems

- Major household accidents (e.g., burns, falls, poisoning, etc.)
- Medical attacks (e.g., asthma), surgical emergencies (e.g., appendectomy) or onset of serious illness
- Serious car accidents in which your child and/or others have been hurt
- Sudden loss of ability to cope (e.g., schizophrenic episode, severe depression)
- Loss of a place to live (e.g., eviction, repossession of home)
- Physical abuse (e.g., husband beating wife. N.B. — The husband may be your son.)
- Serious substance abuse requiring hospitalization and treatment

Your list might be slightly different, but it should not include your son's messy work space or your daughter's weight-loss difficulties; it should not include your grandson's poor grades or your granddaughter's junk food eating habits. These are not defined as crises. You may, nonetheless, have decided that you absolutely have to intervene around something that bothers you terribly, something you feel has or will have awful consequences for your adult child — even if it isn't a crisis. Here are a few guidelines:

- Choose your issues carefully.
- Prioritize; pick one issue that concerns you the most and let the others slide.
- Be creative. Your children are tired of hearing you give them the same old admonitions in the same old way.
- Be prepared not to get your way. Accept the fact that you can go just so far and no further. When you hit a wall — your child's resistance — pack up your magnificent arguments and move on.

Pseudo-Crises

Some people thrive on crises. Crises keep them at a high level of excitement: it may be the only time they feel alive. At any given moment, their lives may seem to be falling apart. Friends and family members may get caught up in the edge-of-disaster embroilments of such a person and, with the best of intentions, try to help. Sometimes they can help and some dire emergency is avoided, but often the help of a loved one only exacerbates the problem. The crisis-prone person may thrive on the attention that crises bring. A certain amount of attention from friends or family will be forthcoming. But when concerned others feel that they are no longer listened to, that their caring doesn't make a dent, they may get discouraged and turn away. At this point, the crisis-prone individual will, very likely, become embroiled in new, accelerating crises and the syndrome will repeat itself.

Crisis-prone individuals are often non-linear in their thinking and behavior and may have trouble with organization and prioritizing. Planning ahead and allotting appropriate amounts of time to projects are also not their strong points. Deadlines are their nemeses. Often, other people come to them with their own problems, sensing that they will be listened to and attended to right away.

It is wise for you as parent to take a step back from your adult child's problems and try to look at his attitude towards his problems. If he is on the brink of crisis all the time, that is where he may want to be. It will be very difficult for you to break into that deep and complex motivational system and simply help him. If crisis mode is a way of life for your child, take a back seat. It is beyond you. As things lie, he doesn't want or can't receive your help.

You might consider, however, a campaign of paying more-than-usual attention to him in ways not related to crises. Invite him over for dinner, suggest a movie, a long hike, an afternoon at a museum, a round of golf. If he talks about the crisis he is involved in, listen attentively and say, "Oh, I'm sorry to hear that." Anything more than that is probably counterproductive.

I have labeled this syndrome a pseudo-crisis. Your adult child doesn't believe what she is suffering is in any way pseudo, and it would be counterproductive if you were to tell her it was. You may come to understand that "crisis" is your child's middle name: you probably cannot break the pattern, but you can keep from aggravating it.

Parental Ego Crises

It was Hillary and Desmond's wedding day. Twenty minutes before the ceremony was to begin, Hillary's mother, June, was checking with the caterers behind the scenes. The wedding cake, a large sheet cake, had been baked the night before and had been boxed and wound with string. June decided to open the box and put the cake out on the food table. She let out a shriek when she saw that the box top had messed up the beautiful cake decoration: "On Your Wedding Day" was now unreadable. June covered her face, uttered some unintelligible sounds of woe, and fell into a chair, distraught. "Oh my God," she moaned, "What a disaster." When a baker came out to see what the trouble was, June began another round of shrieking and hand wringing. "No problem," said the baker, "We'll have that fixed in about five minutes."

Parents who get over-involved in their children's lives — their homes, careers, children, performances, ritual events — can develop an active fantasy life that dictates perfect solutions to everything. The beautiful wedding cake becomes their wedding cake: the disaster is their disaster. Such parents cling to the appearance of crises with relationship-destroying tenacity. It is time to eliminate botched up wedding cake decoration, or anything like it, from one's crisis dictionary.

You might feel an attack of parental ego coming on, let us say, when your adult child has failed to catch a fly ball in a baseball game, allowing the other team to win. You cannot change things. Let him suffer the frustration and disappointment. Let him define it as a performance crisis if he chooses; you do not have to. Your job is to be sympathetic, to say, "Too bad." He will appreciate your involvement but reject your over-involvement. But how can you tell the difference between the two?

Over-involvement is about you — your needs, your embarrassment, your disappointment. It is not about your boundless love for your child. If your child rejects your solicitous concern for his crisis, he is probably sensing that your concern is about yourself, not him. He is telling you that you have gone over an invisible line. When your adult child tells you to back off, listen to him. You have become over-involved!

How and When to Communicate Your Fears to Your Adult Children

As with young children, it is best to communicate your fears when you are not exploding with stress, anger, and frustration. (The exception, of course, is the time-bound, dire emergency — the oncoming car, the falling tree, the fearsome animal.) If you wait until you are reasonably calm you will speak in ways that are less likely to raise your adult child's hackles. You will not say things that you will regret later. You will be able to ease into a sensitive topic instead of blurting out your worries, or worse, screaming invective.

In Chapter 2, I warned against name-calling, interrupting, and talking too much. Nowhere are these rules more vital than when communicating your fears for your child's health or safety or other problems that you see as critical. If you really want to succeed in getting your adult child to stop smoking — an immensely difficult thing to do using the best of techniques — you cannot err too much on the side of casualness, of being soft-spoken, of appearing not to be concerned. You can accomplish this feat, paradoxically, only when you understand fully the limitations of your parent-power — that you have no moral right to change another adult human being, even your child; their habits, behaviors, character traits, and interpersonal style are not yours to manipulate. You will be able to accept the fact that she is a smoker and may continue to be one until or unless something happens to turn her around (and that something, in all likelihood, won't be you). By accepting her as a smoker you are loving her as she is. By knowing that you love her as she is, she may be receptive to taking in and processing anti-smoking messages that abound all around her. Her life with you will be less of a battle of dominance versus autonomy: she will no longer need to thwart you by acts of self-destruction.

This might be a good time to re-read the section on I-statements described in Chapter 2. I-statements are particularly useful when communicating your fears about serious health and safety issues to your adult child. It is counterproductive to say, "How can you continue to smoke, when you know it leads to lung cancer and heart disease?" On the other hand, it may be okay to speak from the heart, using the pronoun "I" to phrase your concern: "I am really fearful for your future when I see you smoke."

If you are able to hold back from expressing your concerns and fears to your adult child immediately, you may also be able to make time for researching the problem. If you suspect your son may be taking recreational drugs on a regular basis or is putting himself at risk for catching AIDS, learn as much as you can about currently available drugs or about AIDS incidence and methods of prevention. Some of what you learn may increase your concern, but some may reduce it. Knowledge reduces the fantasy elements in your thinking and enables you to discuss these topics in public — including with your children — with a minimum of superstition. Your children will respect your clearheaded understanding of the issue of AIDS, for example, and will be less likely to dismiss your opinions and arguments as know-nothing speechifying of the Older Generation.

Giving Advice in Times of Crisis

Giving advice is one of the points of greatest tension and conflict in our relations with our children. Parents want to help their children out of scrapes and difficult situations by telling them how to do it better. But giving advice often makes matters worse.

Heather, 34, was partnered with Sally, 28. They had been living together for three years and were planning a marriage ceremony. Heather wanted a baby very badly and had found a clinic specializing in impregnating lesbian would-be mothers with donated sperm. The problem, from Heather's parents point of view, was that she had no health insurance. Her father, Carl, got on her case without let-up.

"How come your job doesn't provide health insurance? Have you asked them? Are you sure they are not discriminating against you?"

"They're a new company, Dad, and they just haven't gotten it together yet."

"Yes, but you're trying to get pregnant. You have to get insurance before you get pregnant in order to get all your pre-natal and delivery costs paid for. And what if you have some special problem in the pregnancy? Do you realize what that can cost? Tens of thousands!"

"It's okay, Dad, trust me. The clinic is actually very inexpensive and they cover the basics. Everything will be all right. And, anyway, I'm not pregnant yet. It'll all work out."

"But —"

"It'll be fine."

Where did Carl go wrong? Or did he? Carl's approach is probably recognizable to all parents concerned about a situation which could result in financial disaster for their child. However, he could have improved his chances of moving his daughter in the direction of sensible decision-making around money with some changes in his approach.

He needs to be aware that continual questioning is perceived by the person being questioned as invasive. This will turn the listener off.

She will either no longer hear the questions or change the subject or walk out of the room. She will probably not answer such questions honestly. "Everything will be all right" is basically a dishonest answer. It is very different from an answer she would give a friend towards whom she had no animosity and with whom there was no power imbalance. It is a brush-off answer that tells nothing.

Besides the questioning, Carl does too much talking and not enough listening. He engages in the more-is-better system of confrontation, to wit, if you bombard someone with unassailable facts and arguments over and over the listener will sooner or later break down and follow your advice. This is a desperation move. Carl's good arguments and knowledge of relevant facts collapse when he uses them to bludgeon his daughter. If he listened to her story first, and saved his trump cards for the end of the interaction, Heather might be able to hear and to follow his advice.

If Carl is secretly worried that he and his wife will have to pick up the tab in the event of a complication of pregnancy, he should say so. This may be one of the causes of tension and irritability underlying his manner. He may not want to bring this out for fear of appearing selfish in Heather's eyes. If he isn't sure how he would feel about paying for his uninsured daughter, he should express his unsureness. Everyone can understand ambivalence; it is part of our everyday lives. He might have said something like: "If you have a complication of pregnancy or delivery and you get a $25,000 bill from the hospital — which is by no means unheard of — I'm going to be torn about whether I should pay the bill to get you out of a jam or whether I should just let you sink or swim on your own. This is causing me a lot of anxiety. I want to do the right thing, but I'm not sure what the right thing is."

Heather would then have to mull over her father's honest statement of his perplexity and come up with a response. She would also want to do the right thing, partly because her father is modeling conscience and character for her. She might say, "Don't worry, Dad, I will take financial responsibility for everything." If a 34-year-old, able-to-cope individual agrees to financial responsibility for her actions, her parents should honor that pact, come what may.

What, then, are the guidelines for giving advice to our adult children?

- Ask yourself, "Does my child really need my advice?" You may discover, on reflection, that your son's messy home, with unwashed dishes in the sink and mountains of unfolded laundry piling up, is a pattern that works for him. It doesn't hurt him especially nor does it hurt anyone else. You are under no obligation to do his laundry or wash his dishes to alleviate this problem, nor do you have to advise him to get a housekeeper or find some other solution.

- Ask yourself, "Does my child really want my advice?" This is harder than the above because part of you thinks that, whether she wants it or not, she should have it. This is the part of you that needs re-training.

  Marty and Janet, a Caucasian couple, were planning to adopt a mixed-race baby. Janet's parents fretted for months over this decision, thinking of all the potential difficulties for both Marty and Janet and the baby. They discussed this between themselves at great length, and finally decided that their daughter and son-in-law were making this decision with their eyes open and their feet on the ground. They decided to do nothing.

- Trust your intuition. This does not mean acting on the basis of your initial impression. A decision whether or not to give advice requires as much thought and information as you can get. Intuition is not flighty or superficial: it is an expression of our wisest and best selves.

- Differentiate between advice to help your child (e.g., tips on study habits, advice on investing) and advice to alleviate a conflict or sore spot in your relationship (e.g., your ban on smoking in your own home). With the former, ideally, you are a disinterested party. I say ideally because it is really very tempting (and very common) for one's ego to become involved in one's children's study habits, investing practices, or almost anything else. With the latter, the advice may be larded with anger, attempts at punishment, or parental problem-solving. If you tell your child not to smoke in your home you may be subtly advising him not to smoke anywhere while, at the same time, enjoining him to not smoke in your home. If you tell your child not to smoke in your home, you shouldn't be contaminating the instruction with morality. Make it a judgment-free command that says, implicitly, that what he does in his own home, or anywhere else, is not your business. He will appreciate your not judging him, but he will also get a keen sense of your opinion of smoking.

- Give some thought to the thorny issue of embarrassment — yours, not hers. While this may have no relation to a crisis, it is germane to the issue of advice giving. It also crops up at unexpected times and may loom so large as to obliterate more important issues. Your daughter or son may embarrass you in public with her choice of clothes or hairstyle, tattoos or nose ring. She might exhibit behavior that you define as unseemly or rude. She may have personal habits such as loud belching, passing gas noisily, or bathing irregularly which make you want to crawl into the nearest hole. Paradoxically, this might be the perfect place for advice laced with humor. "You'll never get nominated for president with that nose ring. It says so in the Constitution." Humor lets you both laugh together. Humor lets your child know that you still love her, in spite of it all.

  Tackling the issue of embarrassment over your adult child's behavior or appearance is thorny because it forces you to separate from him. You may have thought you had separated long ago, but all of a sudden your son's unkempt appearance causes you embarrassment, anxiety, and, yes, even pain in the presence of your friends. Something tells you that you cannot change him, at least not right now and not with a frontal attack. The only sensible and humane avenue open to you is to let him be himself. Any embarrassment needs to be felt by him, not by you. These are his choices, not yours.

- Finally, your decision to advise or not to advise falls largely on your ability to keep your ego out of the proceedings. Your advice should be for your child and only for your child. He will know if you have a hidden agenda, if your needs rather than his are being reflected in your "advice."

How to Tolerate Seeing Your Child Experiencing Pain

There are many kinds and degrees of pain. Some pain is expressed openly and some is deeply hidden. Some pain we might want to question: Does a blind person who once could see experience pain in not having sight? Do we know whether a seriously overweight person experiences anguish? Should we assume that a person who has lost an elderly parent is experiencing pain? It is a good idea to ponder what some perceived adversity actually means to the other person. It is particularly useful to take time out to try to understand whether your adult child is experiencing pain in the same way you would, or the way that seems likely on first glance.

Psychological pain, unlike physical pain, may have to be inferred. What you imagine as painful may be experienced differently by your children. A break-up with a good friend, for example, may be experienced as a troubling combination of remorse and relief. If you aren't told of your child's feelings you may have no way of knowing. Your first job is to recognize that you don't know. Your second is to commiserate when you do know.

It is important to recognize that over-concern and over-involvement in your adult child's pain often results in your son or daughter refusing to share it with you. Your child does not want to cause you pain: he does not want to feel guilty over your suffering on his behalf. Your high level of concern erases smooth and free-flowing communication between you. Yet, even though it may be a highly personal question, it is possible to ask your adult child if she is in pain or is suffering without being rebuffed. As Stephen Levine has so aptly put it, "love is the optimum condition for healing."[4] The key here is to recognize that you have no automatic right to an answer. It will help if you ask the question humbly and with no intention to fix or manipulate. If you can get yourself to a place — a spiritual place — where your only motive is just to be with your child in her pain, you and she will have a chance to deepen your connection and to establish real adult/adult friendship.

Carrie ached to get the lead role in an off-Broadway production of "The Glass Menagerie." She had studied the part of Laura for weeks, in between stints as a waitress. Her audition seemed to go well. She loved Tennessee Williams and thought she was perfect for the part. At 31, she had done some summer stock and had had a few minor roles on TV: It was time for her to get a break into the Big Time. She shared all this with her parents, Lisa and Harold, who empathized with their daughter's tensions and the ups and downs of her career. They also really liked her acting, and were convinced that she would be discovered, entertaining vivid fantasies of Carrie's fame and fortune to come.

When Carrie failed to get the role, she delivered the news by crying real tears in her parents' living room.

"Mom, Dad, I'm a nobody as an actress and I'll always be a nobody. They just don't like me. I worked so hard on that role, I had just the right southern accent and everything. My agent has nothing new for me, no try-outs, nothing. What kind of a life is waiting on tables forever?" And so forth, into the night.

Carrie's parents found themselves crying with her. They thought of saying ameliorative things such as, "It's not the end of the world," and, "You'll get other parts," but they couldn't mouth the clichés. They held Carrie's hands, put their arms around her, surrounded her on the couch with their sturdy, parental bodies and with their love.

Lisa said, "I'm so sorry to hear it."

Harold said, "Carrie, you are my favorite actress. What's wrong with those turkeys?"

Carrie's tears slowed as she warmed to her parents' solid presence and support.

Physical pain is something else again. It is not easy to see or even know about our child experiencing acute physical pain. One might say that our first role as a parent is to comfort our child in any way we can. But it does not always work out this way. We may be unable to get to our child's bedside. We may be traveling or caring for another family member. We may have to make gut-wrenching priority decisions. We are only human and we do the best we can. We will be better parents if we work at avoiding guilt because we are not doing enough.

Accepting Your Adult Child's Path as a Reality

We get used to many things — a baby born deaf, a teenager who has lost the ability to walk, an adult child who has life-threatening asthma attacks. Adversity happens. The Russian roulette of life and death never ceases to operate. You or your loved one may be driving home from work on that bridge when an earthquake hits and the bridge collapses. Lightning may strike the tree under which your son is standing. We do the best that we can under often baffling and unforeseen conditions. It is the price we pay for human life.

In the previous chapter we discussed self-acceptance as an important ingredient in the formula for establishing friendship with our adult children. We are better able to accept them as they are if we can accept ourselves as we are. In crises, acceptance becomes an even more potent player. Your daughter's auto accident has rendered her paralyzed, unable to take care of herself or to hold a job. She had been a corporation lawyer and a week-end soccer player. Now...

Consider the following: God has given you a gift. The gift is a very special message, available to everyone but not perceived by everyone. Because of the accident, you now know, really know, the preciousness of life, the thinness of the thread that holds us all here, the precariousness of the over-filled rowboat that could sink at any time. Your child is now in a different place in her life trajectory. Your role in her life will necessarily be different from what it was. She has changed and you, as her parent, are being challenged to change. You are being challenged to live in the present, to accept the new reality with grace.

Besides acceptance of misfortune you can also move beyond disapproval. You have struggled, up till now, with your son's drinking, smoking, or drug taking. You have admonished your daughter about her spending habits and her difficulty holding a job. All of these things seemed critical to you and, at times, you felt your child was on the verge of disaster. The least you could do, as a caring parent, was express disapproval.

But take a step back. Consider looking for a new voice, a voice that does not include worry, verbal finger pointing, and premonitions of doomsday. You have raised this child and he has some of your intelligence, your courage, your thoughtfulness, goodness, flexibility, humor, and, perhaps, your drive. Find the qualities in yourself that he shares with you. He will not travel the same path that you have traveled, but he will use some of the traits and values that he has learned from you to persevere, to find the right niche for himself, and to custom design his life around his needs. He will be successful on his own terms and in his own time.

Accepting your adult child's path as a reality also means accepting not always getting your way. Things don't always work out. Be happy when a few of them do. It helps, also, to accept yourself as imperfect. In so doing you will be closer to accepting not only the imperfections of your child but also the thorny ups and downs, the unexpected crises, the little and not so little disasters over which you have no control.

The challenges for parents:

- to remember that what seems like a crisis to you may not be seen that way by your adult child.
- to differentiate between chronic and acute problems.
- to avoid intervention in chronic problems that are not creating immediate crises.
- to recognize acute problems that call for immediate intervention.
- if you must intervene in a chronic problem, to choose one problem only.
- to be alert to crisis-proneness in your adult child.
- to recognize your own over-involvement in your adult child's problems.
- to use I-statements if you decide to give advice.
- to recognize when giving advice is satisfying your needs rather than those of your adult child.
- to be there for your adult child in pain, without feeling that it is up to you to fix it.

6

SHARING

Erasing the Barriers to Engagement Between You and Your Adult Child

> "There are two ways of spreading light:
> to be the candle or the mirror that
> reflects it."   — Edith Wharton

WHEN I WAS A YOUNG ADULT, still smarting from a stormy, breakaway adolescence, my husband and I discovered three shared activities that lessened the tension when my parents came to visit: eating out together, visiting antiques shops and playing bridge. Although, ideally, I would have liked to talk about our relationship problems as well, I couldn't see it working in my family where there was only one right way to do something. Through trial and error, we hit upon certain refinements in our shared activities, such as switching pairs in bridge — the men versus the women, for example — and agreements about bill paying in restaurants. Without our shared activities our touchy relationship would have hardened into a series of no-growth clichés and unwanted judgmentalism and anger.

Sharing activities with your adult children is more than makework. It is the practical stuff of life and the fodder for living relationship. Without sharing at some level, it is hard for parents and children to be friends. Yet we often shy away from sharing. Busy lives and demanding work schedules tell part of the story, but not all. Parents and adult children all too often are alienated from one another. Adult children may not yet have resolved the thorny issues of their adolescent rebellion. Alternatively, they may never have rebelled openly and, hence, may be needful now of establishing their separateness from their parents.

Parents, in turn, may be keenly sensitive to their adult child's need for space, so much so that they are afraid to rock the boat. After many years of poor communication, they are defensive with each other about their carefully molded ideas, behaviors, and lifestyle. They give up — before even trying — on being able to share an activity comfortably and enjoyably.

This alienation may grow and harden with the years without either party defining it as such. But there it is for all to see. Parents and adult children keep themselves from each other, acting as though they don't want, need, or love each other. Alienation leads to not sharing and not sharing, in turn, maintains the alienation.

The relationship between you and your adult children contains a built-in disparity in age, experience, and power. The difference in age and experience is a given, but the power difference, the politics of the relationship, is open to manipulation and change. If parents can find painless ways to relinquish their formerly enormous power over their now-grown children, they will find that alienation dissipates. Sharing becomes a natural outgrowth of love and affection: you will want to share with them and they with you. But to understand how to get there, you will need to take a close look at some of the roadblocks that keep you from achieving your goal.

The Driver's Training Syndrome

Nowhere is parental domination and child submission more stark than when a parent sets out to teach his child something:

- which the parent believes he knows how to do properly,
- which the child wants to learn how to do, and
- which can have serious consequences if it is not mastered.

There is pressure on the learner to take the task seriously and to learn to do it well. Teaching one's son or daughter how to drive is the quintessential example of this. The parent feels justified in exerting authority and in describing, categorically, right ways and wrong ways. There is little, if any, room for creativity or self-expression.

Through trial and error, painful experiences, and cautionary tales, many parents will avoid teaching their teenage or young adult children to drive. They know that the interaction is fraught with danger. They would like to think that teaching them to drive is a good, down-to-earth solution to a common family issue, but it often fails miserably. In truth, the Driver's Training Syndrome is an unacceptable model for many parent/adult child interactions. Teaching your son or daughter how to use power tools, how to ski, or how to install electric wiring may also not work. Why not?

The right way and the wrong way

Throughout life we experience the tension between accomplishing tasks according to some pre-ordained standard of perfection and doing so according to our pleasure, our whim. A four-year-old is allowed to bang on a piano and is not usually given instruction in the right way to do it. We determine that at a certain age she is ready to cope with rules that will allow her, through steady practice, to produce music like her father, her Aunt Greta, or her older brother. She dimly knows the goal, but part of her doesn't want to give up her childish freedom to bang on the keyboard, to create her own music. So strong is the tension that a great percentage of fledgling music students can't cope with the discipline and drop out after a year or two.

Remembering childhood

Adults who have mastered a skill understand the restraint, discipline, and practice necessary to improve or just maintain it. They know where safety precautions and attention to detail are vital. They may not remember what it felt like to be a beginner — the awkwardness and befuddlement, the awesome difficulty of mastery, the continual raising of the bar. An adult child's alienation from his parents can express itself in the tension between his desire to bang on the keyboard, so to speak, thus setting his own rules and standards, and his desire to play competently, based upon well-recognized, public standards.

Even more importantly, your adult child can bang his own keyboard as much as he likes; the standards are being set by him now, not you. In many areas he may choose to be childlike, unschooled, or even incompetent. This is his choice. Let him be.

The issue of trust

Carol's mother, Sandra, was an antique dealer and knew a lot about re-finishing furniture. Carol, aged 21 and living with her parents, wanted to improve the look of an oak chest-of-drawers picked up at a flea market which sported old, dark, blistering varnish. Sandra offered to help Carol with the refinishing job, aware that the stripping compound was fairly toxic and required certain precautions such as opening windows and wearing gloves.

Carol countered with: "I can do it, Mom, it's OK."

Sandra was worried, and persisted. "Look, this kind of work takes some care, some experience. I've re-finished many pieces. It's not hard, exactly, but...Why don't you let me help you get started?"

Carol's voice became icy. "I know what to do, Mom. Don't you trust me?"

This raised Sandra's hackles; she was caught in a trap. She really didn't trust her daughter with paint stripper in her bedroom, at least not without some initial supervision. But Carol was baiting her, testing her. Sandra felt she couldn't take the bait and say, "No, I don't trust you." It would be taken to mean: "I don't respect you," or worse yet, "I don't love you," not to mention, "You're still a kid."

The refinishing job took place with mother hovering nervously, daughter sulking histrionically and an unpleasant atmosphere of tension enveloping the whole process, which lasted for days.

Is there a better way? The simple answer is to try to avoid the repeated temptation to teach your child something that you know well. Doing so can be a subtle form of domination, even if you are convinced it is for your child's own good. When teaching something like driving, the message can easily be communicated that you don't trust your adult child to learn to drive competently and safely. If you cannot contain your fears for your child's safety, avoid taking on the role of teacher, mentor, or authority.

But there are times when you must say No. Whether your adult child is twenty or forty, there are things which you cannot tolerate in your dwelling. Take some time to think about what these things might be. You may have to say, "You may do this, but only if you follow some instructions that I will give you. Otherwise there are too many risks to health, safety, or property damage. I would give these same instructions to anyone, not just you."

By making such a speech at the outset, you take command of a potentially difficult situation, guarding against your own guilt ("I am not trusting my child enough. I'm a bad parent."), and guarding against guilt-producing manipulation by your son or daughter ("Don't you think I'm old enough to figure this out, Dad?").

Your son or daughter will take instruction more readily from a qualified stranger — say, a driving instructor — than from a parent. We all know this to be true but we may not have taken the time to think about why it is so. Why is competitiveness between parent and adult child a major stumbling block on the road to peaceable sharing?

The Scourge of Competitiveness

Much of your guilt and your adult child's alienation derive from the competitiveness which is, arguably, built into the parent/child relationship. Toxic competitiveness can flow from child to parent but also from parent to child. Many games and sports such as chess and football are inherently competitive and tend to lose their edge or interest when competition is lacking. Competition becomes toxic when a father feels compelled to beat his daughter at chess or a daughter needs to prove that she can knit a more beautiful sweater than her mother.

Competitiveness felt by the parent

As with anyone else, parents may carry with them a lifetime of insecurity about their accomplishments, including education and earning capacity. They may see themselves as deficient and, perhaps, too old ever to reach an imagined goal. They may be all too aware of their dearth of knowledge of new technologies or their total lack of experience in certain areas. They may never have learned to swim or ride a bike, for example. If their adult children appear more accomplished than they, parents must sometimes deal with bouts of envy, feelings which may be suppressed or repressed if they are too strong for comfort.

Repressed envy for one's adult child's accomplishments may lead a parent to promote his shortcomings as the right way to be ("Knowledge of high tech is a waste of time," or "Why would anyone want to go mountain climbing, anyway?")

On the other hand, an insecure parent may take a passive, self-denigrating role and endlessly acknowledge his child's superiority. This approach allows the parent to avoid rampant competitiveness, but at the expense of full exercise of his capacities. Furthermore, his view of his child's abilities will tend to be skewed, unrealistic.

Parents and their adult children occasionally compete for the same limited goal, where there is only one winner — they have both entered the same Scrabble competition, for example. This need not be avoided for fear of toxic fallout. Parents and adult children can compete if the competition can be circumscribed, kept within the limits of the game or sport. It also helps if you apply your best kidding-around instincts to the interaction around the competition. Keep it light!

Competitiveness felt by the adult child

Adult children may feel that they can never catch up with their parents, they can never have their parents' experience, wisdom, or hard knocks. Competitiveness with the same-sex parent for the attention and affection of the opposite-sex parent is an underground river that informs behavior throughout life. It does not follow, however, that it is irrelevant to this discussion or unworthy of our attention.

Parents may effectively block off areas of expression or experience for their adult children. Large chunks of life are not considered important by some parents (working-class jobs, for example). Accordingly, parents may refrain from giving recognition to their children for, say, waiting on tables. The adult child, then, feels pressured to show off accomplishments that are acceptable to his parents. Or he may continue with the "unacceptable" job, daring the parent to love him anyway. A simmering hotbed of competitiveness involving values, pastimes, and pursuits has been established.

There are some well-known ways for parents to avoid competitiveness with their adult children, but the one which follows is fraught with danger.

Ego Involvement in Your Adult Child's Activities

We all want our adult children to be rich and famous. Or do we? More importantly, should we?

Eleanor's parents had put her in ballet school at the age of six. She quickly showed a lot of promise and was promoted to a series of more advanced classes. Her mother and father took great pleasure in talking about their daughter's talent to all their friends and relatives. Eleanor started appearing with the other students in recitals which her parents attended with great enthusiasm. In her mid-teens, Eleanor performed a pas-de-deux in a large, public concert hall, for a ticket-buying audience. Mother and father invited everyone they knew and, in fact, twenty-three family members and close friends showed up. The four or five other ballet numbers, and the twenty or so other performers, did not exist for Eleanor's parents. Their total involvement in their daughter's achievement erased all other considerations, including their critical eye.

Eleanor's parents had never asked her if ballet was something she wanted to pursue. The messages she grew up with and lived much of her life with were:

- You are a wonderful ballet dancer.
- It goes without saying that you love ballet dancing.
- It is unthinkable that you would do anything else.
- You make us proud.

Many years later, after her life had taken a different turn, Eleanor confided to a relative that she never really liked ballet.

It is difficult not to invest our own ego in our adult children's achievements, but it is a mistake to think of this as necessary and inevitable. Ego involvement can grow into a monster if we don't reign it in. It is a barrier to friendship with our children, who will understand intuitively that it is something different from — and even antithetical to — love.

If you are excessively involved in your adult children's achievements, you are probably having trouble separating from them. It may be hard for you to differentiate between your child as an extension of yourself and as a separate human being. Furthermore, it is unpleasant to have to admit that you think of your adult child as an extension of yourself. You try to normalize this gripping inner connection, describing it to yourself and others as universal and peppering your conversation with phrases like "parental bonding" and "mother love." But too much involvement in your adult child's achievements means disappointment when they fail to achieve and puts pressure on them to improve. Ultimately, it becomes a message of non-acceptance and a withdrawal of love.

Being trapped in this behavior spells relationship loss for both parents and adult children. Your adult child cannot love what she is doing if the activity is not really hers. And if it is not really hers she will not want to share it with you. It is, at some level, bogus, and she is not unabashedly proud of her accomplishment even if you are, sometimes because you are.

Doing things for your adult child's own good is another variant of ego involvement. When he was a youngster you introduced him to classical music, theater, tennis, repairing lawn mowers, baking bread, and a host of other things to increase his competence and widen his range of abilities. As the parent of a 35-year-old, however, you are in a difficult place, as is he. Your interests and his have had many years to diverge and develop on their own. A host of different influences have brought your son to where he is now, at 35. He may not have glommed onto any of the worlds you presented to him as a child. He may now be a drummer in a rock band; you may think of rock music as undifferentiated noise. The challenge facing you is simple: to accept your son as a rock musician — to love him anyway.

The best way to pass along your enjoyment of a line of work, a skill, or a pastime to your adult child is, first of all, to love what you are doing. Your adult child will absorb your enthusiasm before she learns any technical details. Conversely, trying to teach your child something you don't love but think is good for her is likely to end in failure.

Ego involvement in one's child's achievement, in whatever form, is really the antithesis of sharing. It presumes that parents' lives are defined by their children's accomplishments; that the children's accomplishments are designed to serve the egos of the parents; and that an egalitarian give-and-take does not serve the parents' ego needs.

To sum up, if you really want your adult child to do something well, first examine your motives. Do you want your child to excel because it will reflect on you? Are you compensating for your own failures? Are you beginning to have fantasies about your son or daughter becoming, say, a world-class tennis player? If a healthy relationship with your grown child is your primary goal, let her know that you will love her just as much whether she goes for top honors in tennis or not.

True Sharing Between Parents and their Adult Children

Jerry, aged 61, invited his son Lew, aged 32, to accompany him on a fishing trip. A successful accountant, Jerry loved his deep-sea fishing hobby. He would hire a skipper with a fishing boat and go out for several days, sleeping in the boat's cabin and awakening before dawn to try for an early morning catch. Lew had never gone out with his father; there was a chasm of difference in their experience and ability. Lew also had difficulties with his father who had an authoritarian streak and a penchant for telling his children how to do things.

This trip could be a breakthrough for Lew or it could be a deepening of the old dominance/submission routines that he knew so well. Lew was hoping it would open up an avenue for an adult/adult friendship between him and his father. What he didn't know was that Jerry had been thinking much the same thing. Jerry sensed that Lew wasn't very happy, and that he, Jerry, had something to do with that.

Many times during the trip Jerry had to resist the temptation to give instructions, to explain exactly the right way to bait a hook, cast a line, or reel in a fish. He still was the dominant figure, the experienced fisherman, but he found himself leaving small openings that allowed Lew to feel that it was not critical if he made a mistake. Lew, in turn, felt freer than ever before to ask his dad questions and to respect his father's expertise without feeling that it reflected on his own ineptness. Both father and son took home fine memories and the beginnings of an adult/adult relationship.

I have spoken of feelings and behaviors which, taken together, keep joyful parent/adult child sharing at bay. It is useful to focus on two of these — alienation and competitiveness — to see how they impinge on your life.

Ask yourself:

- Am I locked into a competitive struggle with my adult child?
- Do I experience my adult child as an extension of myself?
- Do I really care about my adult child's accomplishment and performances for his sake, or am I concerned with my own greater glory?
- Does my child sense that I really care more about how his behavior affects me than how it affects him?
- Does the thought of sharing activities with my adult children seem like a burdensome task, well-nigh impossible and better avoided?

You may want to come back to these questions over and over again and wrestle with one or more of them. In making breakthroughs to self-understanding you will also begin to see your adult child more clearly. You will begin to get a handle on why she seems to you sullen, closed-mouthed, and lacking in warmth. It is important to keep in mind that your adult child wants to be closer to you, and would prefer not to be sullen, closed mouthed or cold. However, she is feeling pressure, and that pressure pushes her away to where it is safe. She would prefer to share and so would you.

Let's have a look at how you can begin to break down the barriers to sharing:

- With Sunday newspaper in hand, make a list of events of the week that you think your adult child would like to attend and that you would find, at the least, interesting.

- You must make the first moves. De-alienation takes determination, careful thought, and work. Your initial aim is to invite your adult child to accompany you to an event at your expense — an event that both might enjoy.

- Don't be discouraged if you get No for an answer from your child the first few times. She may be busy or under the weather, or stuck in the cliché that parents are old fogies and inhabit a world of out-of-date tastes. Or she may be testing your sincerity. Keep trying!

Your biggest hurdle is to find a way in which you and your adult child can be equals.

Make no mistake. In spite of busyness and, sometimes, an appearance of cool indifference, adult children crave one-on-one interaction with a parent. Family get-togethers are not a substitute for an activity shared between the two of you. Your adult child would love to have an idealized version of your undivided attention. That is, she would like you to really listen, not give unsolicited advice or nag. This apparently simple prescription is just about the hardest challenge in this book. The best way to start the uphill climb is to imagine yourself as a young adult with your own parent. Was he or she able to listen to you without giving advice, without figuring out the solution to your problem before you started to think about it, without nagging?

Getting along with your adult child often entails doing something positive together, something that both of you enjoy. There are ways you can minimize the power and experience differences between you while acknowledging that you may have something new to offer him. No matter how good your intentions, however, you may still see yourself as superior in maturity, understanding, competence, and wisdom. Your biggest hurdle is to find a way in which you and your adult child can be equals.

You may want to seek support at a spiritual level for this position from the Judeo-Christian tradition. The presumption of the equality of all human beings under God is a major tenet of this tradition. It teaches that we are made in the image of God, therefore we are more alike than different — indeed, we are basically the same.

Recent findings in genetics, furthermore, tell us that we humans are more than 99 percent alike genetically. The presumption of equality between any two human beings is not farfetched; it is a manageable and sensible idea with a biological underpinning.

As a spiritual exercise, hold a very young baby, perhaps your own grandchild — ponder it, study it, feel its babyness. Then try to experience that baby and yourself as equals — essentially the same, going through life's awesome journey at slightly different, though overlapping, periods.

You might try the same experiment with a five-year-old. Here, you may be able to remember yourself at this age — your first (scary) day in kindergarten, straining your neck as you looked up into standing adult's faces and clutching your much-loved Teddy bear which you didn't want to share. It may be easier to identify with and therefore feel equal to the five-year-old. You can begin to access this feeling of being equal and apply it to your adult child. Getting in touch with that oneness, the spiritual equality of all human beings, will open a new dimension in your relationship with your adult child. It will infuse everything you do together with ease and mellowness — and pleasure!

Even more exciting, once you have made spiritual equality your own, a teacher/student or a teacher/apprentice relationship between you and your adult children can be marvelously rewarding, useful, and fun. You need not avoid temporarily unequal involvements if your basic outlook is one of equality. The keys to success here are the same regardless of whether you are teaching your daughter chess or electrical wiring:

- Gear the speed of instruction to the abilities of the adult child
- Regularly check in with her:
  - Do you understand?
  - Do you have any questions?

    — Am I going too fast or too slow?

    — Do you want to review anything?

    — Have you had enough for today?

- Avoid condescension. If the above questions seem condescending, ask yourself whether you would appreciate a classroom teacher asking you whether you understand or whether you have any questions. Sure, you would.

- Avoid being doctrinaire. Make note of the multi-sidedness of your subject whenever possible; be open to different ways to accomplish a goal. If you can honestly say to your child, "Oh, that's an interesting way to make a meat loaf. I never thought of that," you have accomplished light years of repair work on your relationship.

- Regularly give her positive input regarding her grasp of the material.

Fran's son, Joel, a graduate student in history, was a computer whiz. Fran, aged 52, couldn't get started with her new, state-of-the-art computer, although she wanted to. She had taken a two-hour introductory class in word processing at her local library, but as soon as she sat down to do the simplest thing, like turn the computer on, she messed up. She was beginning to feel that everyone in the world was able to handle computers but her. When Joel came home on vacation, Fran decided to ask him to give her a crash course. She even offered to pay him. She told him of her misgivings, her fears of permanent incompetence.

"You'll do just fine, Mom. It's easy, once you get certain basics under your belt. You've just got to put in a little time at it. How about right now?"

Fran was surprised and happy to learn that her son was an excellent teacher, that she could ask him as many questions as she needed to, and that he never made fun of her beginner status. For his part, he had a blast showing off his computer smarts, helping out his mom and repaying her for all the things she had taught him.

If you can teach your child some skill, it may be a fine idea to figure out something that your child can teach you. Although this is an excellent overall strategy for improving relations, it need not be seen as an obligation. On the contrary, learning a new skill or body of information from your child can be a rich, joyous experience. You may find yourself learning about electric guitar, rock climbing, vegetarian cooking, or calculus —and in the process gaining serious respect for your child's mastery. The value to your adult child of having a chance to teach you a skill that he knows well is inestimable.

Are there some activities that work better than others as vehicles for connecting with your adult child? Not really, for family members' histories, skills, and interests range very widely. With the obvious exceptions of sexual abuse and behaviors harmful to others, you should embark on any shared activity or project which brings both of you pleasure and satisfaction. There are few inappropriate activities as such, only inappropriate attitudes and behavior regarding the activity. Among these are your need to be better than your child, to show your child up, to set standards of perfection which your child is not likely to reach, and to fail to acknowledge your child's gains or improvement.

Though recommending specific activities may limit your imagination and stunt your creativity, you may want to consider the following:

- Be aware that the distinction between the value of participatory vs. spectator sports and pastimes is often a false one. If watching a football game on TV with your 27-year-old son engages you completely and gives you both a sense of togetherness, then that is the right activity for you. But don't forget live football games — high school, college, and professional — as well as throwing a football in the street, as other ways for you and your son or daughter to share a meaningful block of time.

- Intersperse planned family activities with spontaneous ones. There is nothing to equal a room filled with easy laughter, or group singing that just starts and won't stop. Special moments are even more special when shared with your adult children.

- Be creative: allow your imagination to soar. Even if a project is too expensive or too time consuming, playing with the idea may lead to something do-able.

- If the cost of suggested activities is prohibitive for either of you, suggest a cost sharing arrangement. Decide beforehand what sort of arrangement you are willing to accept. Remember, money issues can produce guilt reactions. Do not offer to pay for your grown child's part of your shared vacation if you suspect your offer will make him feel guilty (he owes you a lot already) or prideful (he really prefers to be independent, no matter what he has to deny himself.)

- If your adult child lives nearby, consider learning something together where you both are starting at ground zero (e.g., Chinese cooking, car maintenance, upholstery, Hebrew, bridge). Choose something about which you are both enthusiastic. Plan to help each other study, work on each other's cars together, or jointly do an upholstery project. If you sense unwelcome competition entering the picture, ask yourself if it's caused by your behavior. Are you being pushy, impatient, critical, or perfectionist when your son or daughter contributes to the project? Are your standards unrealistic, not only for your child but also for yourself? Do you always know — and express — the right way to do everything?

Sharing a project with your adult child is an excellent way to work on interpersonal skills. Above all, keep in mind that such an activity can be an end in itself. Laughing at your seriously off-base French pronunciation with your daughter (who is a beginner just as you are) may enrich your life fully as much as a proper Gallic accent. If your child laughs with you it is a we-are-in-this-together laugh. Cherish it. But resist the temptation to laugh at her.

Ways to Enrich Your Life with Your Adult Children

By now I hope you have begun to feel comfortable with the state of mind which allows true sharing to take place. In the section following I present five categories — major ways of seeing, acting, and organizing the world around us. Each category is intended to serve as a grid or catch-all, both an opportunity for change and a series of tools and understandings for sharing.

From a slightly different perspective, these five pathways will allow you to be with your adult child in rich, creative, ongoing ways. None of them requires special skills but they do require an enhanced ability to live in the present and to seize the moment. Experiment with one or more of these pathways. You may hit upon a rewarding and fulfilling route to friendship.

As with other lists in this book, this one is not exhaustive. It is intended to stimulate your imagination around the multiple joys lying in wait as you move through midlife and approach elderhood. Adding your own life categories to the list will increase its potency and usefulness.

Nature

> *How many parts of this space already were within me!*
> *There's many a wind like a son to me.*
> *Do you know me, air, full of places where I used to be?*
> — *Rainer Maria Rilke*[1]

The natural world is a setting for intimacy. It need not be scary, remote, foreign. Being in the wilderness invites us to drop pretense. We cannot control wilderness unless we cut down every tree, pave over every creek, dam every river. Even then, our efforts are overwhelmed by the power of wind and weather, cold and heat. In nature we are part of the forest, the plain, the challenging mountain path. We take nature to us and allow nature to embrace us. Nature can be awesome but it isn't necessarily beautiful — it just is! We are part of that "is" if we allow ourselves to be embraced. Everything in nature is moving along the unstoppable path of its own survival, its own fulfillment. We share that forward thrust with every plant, every creature. Consequently, we are not alone!

Nature is a setting for giving up our egos, for renunciation. In nature we are chastised, humbled, and warmed. How? We don't judge the pebble for being small, the grass for being parched, the tree for being twisted. Similarly, nature doesn't judge us. We can be calmly and gently, yet profoundly at home in nature. We, too, may be small or twisted, but here we are utterly accepted.

We can be intimate with God in the natural world, and with ourselves, our own unjudged selves. We can also be intimate with another human being. Without calling it by name, we can be aware of God's presence. What more natural time and place to share our best selves with another than in the wilderness!

Being in nature with your adult child can mean walking around a lake, climbing a rocky hillside, picking up shells on a quiet beach, or paddling a canoe on an isolated river. It is good to be alone together. The intimacy of silence can be just as nurturing and healing as the intimacy of honest speech. Beware of over-planning: a spontaneous walk in the woods is as enriching as an elaborate vacation, perhaps more so.

Poetry

Poetry is a way of seeing. It is accessible to everybody, even to those who claim not to like or understand it. Poetry is seeing the world with fresh eyes at every moment. It is the opposite of advertising hype, air-filling chit-chat, etiquette as a way of life, ironclad formalities. It encourages boldness without fear, disagreement when your insides tell you No, humor that rises up, bubbling with jollity before disappearing.

Poetry is metaphor. Every sunset we see is different. Yesterday you saw an inverted blue bowl with a delicate, peach porcelain edge; today you see a giant pink powder puff flattening itself against the earth. You didn't write your metaphor down but you spoke it aloud, sending it outward into the universe. You incorporate poetic imagination into your life as your feelings, visions, and needs change.

Poetry as a way of seeing is never finished. It may follow you into the bathroom and to the breakfast table, and it is a major player in your dreams. It is equally available to your adult children and to you. It is something you and your children can share.

Some people are a little afraid of poetry, and so avoid reading or writing it. If that is true in your family, you and your adult children may be free to approach the subject without preconceptions. You may both engage in creating poetry with no rules except those you decide upon together. You may get into humorous haiku or sexy limericks. You may paint word pictures of a crowded, urban street, a snow-capped peak, or the autumn leaves falling outside your window. Actually, you are tired of saying, "Oh, what a beautiful day" yet again. Your adult child is as tired of the automatic response as you are. Add poetry to your lives together by substituting heightened expression of feeling for bland agreeableness.

When you and another express yourself on any subject keenly and pointedly, harvesting the words from the truth cavities of your heart, something warm and wonderful can happen: You discover that you don't need to be talking all the time. You can experience each other in silence with a sense of connectedness and amplitude. Your silence together does not represent fear of saying the wrong thing. It is not the silence of repression, of unrealized relationship. It is the silence that grows from each one allowing the other to be fully herself.

Poetry is not confined to books of poems. All good fiction is larded with poetry. Plays and song lyrics can be mined for new ways of seeing familiar things. One way to start bringing poetry into your life is to write a poem to your adult child on a special occasion, perhaps his birthday. In your own humorous or lyrical — but absolutely unique — style, you can tell him how well you love him.

Making pictures

Our eye/brain connection has the awesome capacity to make pictures. It can do this at any time. All of these images are unique and original to each of us. We may not pay heed to these visual wonders, yet they are there for the taking if we are blessed with sight. (Another, similar connection — brain/memory — paints pictures for us in our sleep.) We can make pictures in a number of ways, but the most accessible is to frame striking images and views that pass across our visual spectrum. Sometimes a window frames a scene for us, at home or in a moving vehicle. If it is particularly colorful or balanced or dramatic, we find ourselves saying, "It looks just like a picture postcard." But no! The postcard imitates our eyes, our way of seeing, not the other way around.

If we want to preserve what we see we draw or paint or photograph our world. We produce a testament to our intense connection with that world. While there are well known standards of quality and beauty, no one can divorce us from our subjectivity and from our expression of that subjectivity on paper or canvas or any other medium. Whether or not we display our pictures publicly, they are part of our lives. We can share our picture making with others, and in particular, with our adult children.

In seeking ways of being equal, your family may take up picture making (as other families take up poetry) as a field in which neither you nor your adult child has special skills or pretensions. Again, you are both starting at ground zero. That lightweight, fairly expensive camera that is gathering dust in a drawer may be a good place to start. The next time you and your son or daughter travel together, even if it's only for a picnic in the park, take that camera with you and do a few things that you probably have never done before. First, forget about taking endless photos of your son standing next to a tree, facing the camera and smiling. Instead, take in the beauties around you and use the viewfinder to frame a scene that strikes you as particularly lovely. Think of yourself as an artist, even if you have never thought of yourself this way before. Snap only pictures that, in your estimation, should be preserved on film. Most important of all, share the camera with your adult child. In this way, when you examine your prints, neither of you will quite remember who took which pictures. Relive your time together by examining the prints and delighting in how well some of them came out. Make a simple album or collage to commemorate your time together and your picture-making project (or, make two — one for you and one for him).

The activities listed above can be amended to fit other art projects — making clay bowls or block-print greeting cards, for example. Both you and your adult child will have to free yourselves from the notion that you have no artistic ability and that the project is therefore doomed to failure. A good way to escape this trap is to try to remember what it was like in kindergarten or first grade. In early-childhood classrooms, any sensitive teacher encourages all children to enjoy the process. Whatever the result, it represents your effort, your labor, and your imagination. And your teacher probably found words to praise your work.

Around fourth or fifth grade, however, teachers and pupils alike decide who in the class can really draw. Some 10-year-olds with keen visual memory are beginning to master the human body, a horse in action, perspective. But why close off the wonderful world of picture making — and other art production — because later teachers and other adults failed to encourage your efforts? You can take a step towards expressive freedom at any age. But, even more exciting, you can encourage your adult child to take the step with you. You can open yourself up to a new expressive language while, at the same time, strengthening and enriching your relationship.

Making music

Music relates deeply to the human body — and, therefore, to movement and dancing. The regularity of walking, running, clapping, and even our heartbeats are reflected and elaborated in drumbeats and other rhythms. The ability of our voices to produce varying pitches allows us the wondrous joy of producing melody, which we can embellish with melody's complex partner, harmony. Music is embedded in all cultures and subcultures. It can be a mating call; it can carry a political message; it can tell a lyrical, comic, or tragic story; it can inspire national pride; it can help to ease pain; it can engage and integrate body, mind, and spirit; it can bring disparate people together with an enhanced sense of belonging.

And yet many people have given up on making music — singing, playing, listening, learning. They may have become convinced that they can't carry a tune. (They speak very much the same language as those who have rejected "art" because they "can't draw a straight line.") They are missing out on one of life's supreme joys. At the age of five they did not know of the concept of "talent," and therefore had no sense of their relative ranking on a scale of musical ability. They just sang, danced, played rhythm instruments, and listened to music at home or school. Can disaffected grownups find a way to enjoy music again? If so, how? And how does all this pertain to parents and adult children?

Getting back on the musical track can, oddly enough, be facilitated by becoming aware of the age-graded nature of popular musical taste. People over 60 may not care for rock music, and may have no connection whatever with rap. Very often, we form our lifetime musical tastes in our teens and early 20s, and have dozens of familiar numbers etched on our memories. My mother, Henrietta, age 93 at this writing, is buoyed up with pleasure upon hearing songs like "When You Wore a Tulip" and "Down by the Old Mill Stream" which were probably old favorites when she was a girl. But the Beatles, Simon and Garfunkel, and even Stephen Sondheim are a foreign language to her. Too bad! Mutual enjoyment of outstanding music of all genres and eras connects people and can make them feel part of a larger whole.

Trying to understand, appreciate, and even like your son's or daughter's music has several things to recommend it:

- In caring about something that means a lot to her, you are, by extension, noticing, appreciating, and caring about her.
- You may find a branch of her music that you really like.
- She may show an interest in the music of your youth, or in opera or jazz or chamber music. Your music is no longer as threatening.
- It enhances the possibility that the two of you can enjoy music together.

If you struggled, or even suffered, through piano or violin lessons as a youngster, you are not alone. Many grownups took music lessons for many years, only to find that the self-discipline demanded of them was too much. They finally made a break and, sadly, abandoned the instrument. Then the cycle may have been repeated with their children.

Why wait another moment to enjoy music? You may be able to enjoy this most passionate and satisfying of expressive languages with your adult child. Here are a few ideas to get you started. Use them to stimulate your imagination. Add a custom-made idea to the list that you think would really work for you.

- Get a book of rounds to add to the ones each of you already knows. Sing rounds (with or without a third voice) while walking, sitting around the living room, preparing a family meal together — virtually anywhere. Laughter at your mistakes is inevitable!

- Do family karaoke. Each person gets to sing a favorite solo with taped or live accompaniment. Project words on a screen or hand them out. Each person gets free rein to show off, indulge in histrionics, become a sultry jazz singer or an aggressive rap artist. And each participant is free to make a fool of himself in front of sympathetic family members.
- If someone at a family gathering plays piano or guitar, others can play drums or other rhythm instruments (a pot and spoon will do in a pinch). Get an uninhibited orchestra going at a get-together or celebration. Children and adults alike can sing, dance, and laugh together. It's win/win for everybody.
- If the previous listing sounds too much like pre-school, try this: Invite your adult child to a concert featuring a type of music that is unfamiliar to you both — country fiddling, Klezmer, or jazz choir, for example. If you both enjoy this new musical experience — or even if you both dislike it — you have found a new basis for connection and understanding.
- Ask your adult child if he would like to invite you to a musical event that means a lot to him. Go with an open mind and don't be in a great hurry to pass judgment on it.

Body work

Walking, dancing, and sports of all kinds are available to all who enjoy the power of locomotion. Climbing a mountain (or negotiating a modest-size hill) gets our bodies going and clears out our minds, leaving more room for ad lib poetry, for brook following, for chipmunk spotting, and for pine tree sniffing. A vigorous hike stretches us, sometimes humbles us, helps us to leave our egos behind. We know that the actively engaged body produces chemicals that enhance our mental health. Our hearts stay young through exercise. Everything benefits.

Taking a climb, a hike, or just a walk with your adult child is a form of bonding. You are sharing the outside world, the body-stretching experience and each other's company. You may be sharing, also, trail mix, water bottles, and sandwiches, as well as unforeseen adventure, bad weather, or a medical emergency. All shared adventure — good or bad — brings people together. Bad memories lose their sting over time and modest disasters may become opportunities for shared laughter. Vivid memories, recalled and rehashed for years, are an added bonus to the shared experience.

Sports play a huge role in some people's lives. The field is a large one, from individual stamina and fitness sports such as swimming and biking, to individual, competitive sports such as tennis, to team sports such as basketball and soccer. We have a wonderful array of possibilities for coming together with our adult children, especially since some sports, such as swimming, are both healthful and still possible in one's 60s and beyond.

Gazing out on the street from my ground-floor living-room window I see fathers and sons (some teenage, some older) playing touch football in the street. They are being guys together, calling out moves, yelling encouragement, proving their muscle, showing ancient signs of courage and fearlessness. Not exactly intimate, this testing of one's mettle. It is a different language altogether from sharing of one's soul.

I recall my husband and my older son, Ben, talking baseball trades and statistics, grappling with questions like "Who do you think is going to win the Pennant?" I sometimes wondered just what they got out of it. What about all the other weighty and stimulating subjects available? Why should two intelligent, grown men spend serious time on things that never got resolved? Things that didn't help make the world a better place? Things that never helped them personally? It defied rational analysis. It seemed less important than inner work, sharing one's secrets, intimacy. Yet, there it was — a clear and powerful bonding that was available to men, and sometimes women, at almost any time, any place.

The meta-sport of baseball talk and the real-time sport of touch football are somehow outside of subjectivity; one is all statistics and objective data; the other, losing oneself in the immediacy of running to catch an odd-shaped ball on the fly. Both activities have the capacity to engage the players in immensely compelling, although arguably superficial ways.

Don't underestimate the capacity of sports and outdoor activities to bring you and your adult children together. The exhilaration following a pick-up game of Frisbee, a bike ride around a reservoir, or a short but strenuous rock climb can level some of the tiffs and tensions that have been bedeviling the relationship lately. Sports are not a substitute for honest talk. But sports can help to dislodge some of the soul's poisons, which in turn will make honest talk flow more freely.

The physical activities that you share with your adult child depend on each of your preferences and inclinations, naturally, but consider the following:

- Remember when you played ball with your child when he was a year old, rolling a ball across a few feet of floor so he could catch it between his legs while sitting down. You were gearing the game to his limited skill. You were probably smiling or laughing, and so was he. You probably didn't exactly show him how to do it, try to improve his skill, or act severe if he made an error. Think about how you can incorporate some of your early parenting tricks into physical activities with your adult child.

- Often, your thirtysomething child is stronger, faster, and just plain better than you at tennis or mountain climbing. It's okay. Both you and she have to learn about the body's gradual slowing down. She has to find ways of relating to you on the mountainside that are understanding but not condescending, and you can help her. Humor and a light touch work wonders. "Hey, girl, listen up. Before you know it you will be where I am, so give me a break."

- As with other categories touched on in this chapter, think of some sports or other physical activities in which both of you start off on a level playing field. Neither of you knows anything about Tai Chi, but you know people who swear by it and it sounds intriguing. You and your adult child, assuming you live in the same vicinity, might plan a series of introductory classes together. Neither of you is showing off your prowess to the other, nor are you setting yourselves up for unnecessary or unwanted competition. Your approach is exploratory, the activity is new and different, and you will have another shared experience to talk about together.

- Don't reject competitive sports out of hand, however. Tennis, golf, or pick-up basketball games might work well in your family. The trick is to avoid competition when it is not an inherent part of the activity. There is no need, for example, to compete to see who can best sail a sailboat, catch the most fish, or learn the steps to folk dances quicker.

The challenges for parents:

- to ponder your adult child's alienation from you, and to consider its sources.
- to think about how this alienation affects your ability to share.
- to understand how the Driver's Training Syndrome operates in your life.
- to avoid teaching your child something when you can't trust him to do it safely.
- to determine when you need to say No to an activity in your home and to do so clearly and firmly.
- to understand your feelings of competitiveness with your adult child; to get in touch with your envy.
- to imagine your adult child's feelings of competitiveness toward you.
- to encourage your adult child to do what she really loves, not what you think she ought to love.
- to understand that over-involvement in your adult child's accomplishments may be antithetical to love.
- to invite your adult child to an event you think you both will enjoy; to persevere until you find one he will accept.
- to presume an equality between you and your adult child. If you can accomplish this, teaching or mentoring your adult child can be rewarding and fun.
- to let the natural world envelop you and your adult child, somewhere, somehow.
- to find ways to bring poetry into your lives together.
- to share the visual world with your adult children. Consider moving on from sharing what you see to actual picture making.
- to find a musical language (and a musical activity) that works for both of you.

When all else fails, throw a Frisbee with your adult children and let the healing begin.

7

INDEPENDENCE

The Competing Needs of Parents and Adult Children

Daughter am I in my mother's house
But mistress in my own.
— Rudyard Kipling

RAISING CHILDREN means bringing helpless babies to a state of adult independence and autonomy. But many things conspire to keep the child tied to the home, physically and psychologically, long after adulthood is supposed to have set in. Not the least of these is the high cost of living in post-industrial societies, particularly the costs of housing and education. What is the thoughtful parent's responsibility concerning the provision of financial support, living quarters, subsidies for education or health care for the adult child?

The factors that influence your decisions are complex. You may secretly want your adult child to live at home to provide emotional support and stave off loneliness, especially if you are a single parent. You may be all too aware of the specter of homelessness, of the paycheck-to-paycheck financial status of many young adults and families, prone to topple at any time if, say, an engine overhaul is needed on the family car. You may have invested your own ego in your child's social status — yet you may also see the virtue of letting him sink or swim out there in the real world. You may have a lingering wish to exercise control over your adult child's behavior, even as the first gray hairs appear at his temples.

And, finally, you may disagree with the permissiveness that has permeated child-rearing practices since World War II. The Western

131

world is more child-centered than when you were growing up. The new permissiveness may have economic roots, allowing children-cum-adults to "bum around" — to travel, to take odd jobs, to make education an on-again-off-again affair and to cover some of the empty spaces with drug use — until such time as they can be usefully absorbed into the economy. Even though this is part of a generational change that is all around us, you may still have some difficult decisions to make — whether or not, and how, to set boundaries, for example.

Responsible parents who are used to helping their kids out of a myriad of difficult situations may feel ambivalent when their children are adults. Financial aid — to give or not to give — is one of the most perplexing of parental decisions. We are painfully aware that money-crunch issues have been exacerbated in this era of a rising cost of living. The parental generation bought a house for $30,000 twenty-five years ago. The offspring cannot afford the present-day price of $250,000 for a comparable home, and may never be able to own property. Hard working, two-income couples in their 20s are in a serious financial bind if they yearn for the middle-class amenities that their parents were able to acquire in the post-World War II period. The younger generation can and, it may be argued, should ask for help from their parents.

And yet — and yet — the haunting voice of Emersonian self-reliance and frontier toughness that informs our collective unconscious, makes us squirm. "No," says the voice in our heart. "To be adults means to be able to cope: you must go it alone."

Clearly, some of our decisions concerning financial support come from cultural/ethnic sources. Your own biography and ethnicity have permeated your ideas and values, giving you a sense of right and wrong. People of good will have different views, absorbed when they were growing up, about helping (or not helping) their adult children. It is important to recognize these familial, cultural, and ethnic influences even if you decide to act in ways that run counter to them. You will understand where you are coming from and know that you are not alone.

The world over, families take in their adult children, if they can, to tide them over the difficult early adult period. Extended families function as an economic support group for adult children, and sometimes grandchildren, grandparents, aunts and uncles and cousins as well. In non-Western countries and in countries where poverty is endemic, extended families and multi-generational households are necessary for survival. In Israel and in the disputed territories, for example, Palestinian families build large, block-like homes to house ten to fifteen family members, including adult children and their offspring who may remain there indefinitely. Israeli Jews, similarly, will often provide lodging in their home for their young adult children as they are working toward financial independence. Asking our adult children to fend for themselves may be peculiar to the American middle class, deeply impregnated as it is with the Protestant ethic of self-reliance.

Polly, a woman in her thirties, recently married, had just had a beautiful baby girl. Her husband, Tom, was a middle-level corporate executive and Polly managed a high-tech office. Polly stayed home with her baby for four months but would have liked it to be at least a year, but she thought that she would lose her job if she stayed out any longer. She felt that the family needed two salaries, even though Tom had a high-paying job. Tom's parents were affluent and could well afford to give or loan their children the money to allow Polly to stay home with her baby — but their Protestant heritage produced a self-reliance mindset. It never occurred to them to contribute a significant amount of money to their children.

Webster's Dictionary defines independence as "complete exemption of dependence upon others; self-maintenance, self-government." And further, "property or income sufficient to make one independent of others." Maybe so. But growing up in the century of psychoanalysis we have become immersed in the concept of interdependence. We are rightly skeptical of the possibility of "complete exemption from dependence upon others." We know that this is a very complicated issue with dark caverns of unexamined need. There are adults all around us, furthermore, who are psychologically and financially dependent on parents, who never grow up. Webster's definition doesn't deal with ethnic differences, either. It merely presents us with the goal, the ideal: complete exemption from dependence on others.

Notwithstanding the issues that make this a daunting goal to reach, I take a vigorous stand against dependency even when it seems to satisfy both party's needs. The goal of parenting should be to raise children who can be independent. In the remainder of this chapter, I will try to explicate this goal as it relates to our relationship to our adult children.

Financial Support: When and When Not to Give It

The goal of parenting should be to raise children who can be independent.

Jennifer's daughter, Jody, 29, was a beginning hairdresser in a distant city. Jennifer, 57 and divorced, struggled with her daughter's financial instability and was conflicted and anxious about her own role. She received a phone call from her daughter which, like many of Jody's phone calls, ended up being about money.

"Mom. Hello. Guess what? I was just talking to a new client. She wants me to cut and color her tomorrow after work. Isn't that great?"

"That's terrific. What can you get for that?"

"Well, maybe fifty. I don't know."

Jennifer didn't like herself asking the money question. It would have been sweeter to just say, "That's terrific," with no souring afterthoughts. But this dialogue had a history. It wasn't all perfect.

"Listen, Jody, you need $750 a month to live, right?"

Several seconds went by. Jennifer could feel the hackles rising, hear the silence. Jody was framing her answer — a compromise, perhaps, between "It's none of your business," and "Yes, Mom, you're right on the button."

"Everything's under control, Mom," was what she said.

"But you're only making $400 at the salon, sweetie. That doesn't even pay your rent. It sounds to me like you need to get a restaurant job one or two nights a week, and even that —"

"Mom, listen," said Jody. "I'm a little tired these days. I mean I'm not eighteen or twenty-one anymore. I'm needing to keep myself in good shape so I'm really there when they need me at the salon. I know they like my work and very soon, but I don't know how soon, I'll get put on the floor and be able to do what I know I'm really good at — hair styling. I just can't muddy up the waters with tiring night-time jobs."

"But how are you going to earn enough to live?", Jennifer asked.

"Mom, it'll be okay. Trust me."

Jennifer had just finished paying for her daughter's tuition for a ten-month stint at hair styling school. She felt good about doing it because Jody seemed to be serious and focused about her occupational future for the first time since graduation from high school. She kicked in Jody's rent some months, paid her health insurance, and once or twice paid her long-standing consolidated loan payment of $144. This last was different from Jody's other expenses in that it was in Jennifer's name, and her house was its collateral. Jennifer had nasty daydreams about forfeiting her house to prove a point.

Jennifer has been struggling not only with money issues but with the larger issue of how deeply to involve herself in her adult daughter's life. In this instance, Jody did not ask for money nor did she bring up the subject, but Jennifer felt compelled to do so. She was happy to set Jody up with the promise of a livelihood. The unwritten pact was that Jody would do her best in school and not sabotage her chances of suc cess. But Jody has now finished school, and Jennifer has to disengage. The act of disengaging from a dependent young adult can be fully as problematic for the parent as for the offspring. This is especially true when the newly independent son or daughter backslides and asks for money, wants to live in Mom and Dad's home for an unspecified period, or requests some other form of support.

Jennifer got practice in disengagement when Jody wrote her a letter and asked for help paying for a very overdue parking ticket. Jody's letter was warm and chatty but had a surprise ending:

"P.S. I forgot to tell you I have a parking ticket from Feb. or March. It's on my old dresser. Could you pay it PLEASE mom?? Love ya!"

Jennifer felt a wave of resentment surging through her. The four-month-old parking ticket would be at least $100, maybe closer to $200.

"Who does she think she is, hitting me up for that kind of money, asking me to cover for her irresponsibility?"

Jennifer couldn't just say No — not yet — but she couldn't get the parking ticket out of her mind. Then it hit her; it was that old enemy guilt. Or, to put it another way, it was her difficulty in saying No to Jody's request. Why was it so hard? Was she afraid of Jody's rejection, anger, failure to love her? That was part of it, certainly. But she was also haunted by her knowledge that she, Jennifer, had sufficient funds to pay this ticket and Jody didn't.

Jennifer didn't rush into making a decision. Instead, over the next few days, she pondered her feeling about money, her guilt, and her love for Jody. Her exploration of her feelings about money was the most dramatic. She discovered that she wanted/needed her money for her own security and for her old age. She wanted her money because she had earned it. She wanted her money because she had paid her dues and now she wanted to have a little fun. She wanted her money because she had raised two children and they were grownups now. She wanted her money because it was hers!

Jennifer's revelations were surprisingly guilt-free. She felt relieved and excited. She also had no problem knowing just what to do. She ended her next letter to Jody:

"I'm enclosing the parking ticket you spoke of. I'm sure you will be able to pay it. Too bad you forgot about it till now. Love, Mom."

I have elaborated on Jennifer's struggles because there are a number of lessons embedded in the story. Let's look at them closely. I encourage you to examine my views critically, to find what is appropriate to your particular needs, and to concentrate on those points that are most troublesome for you.

Don't assume beforehand that helping in a particular instance is bad or good. There is no textbook formula for when to help and when not to help your adult children. There are times when offering help is completely appropriate and affirming to all concerned. The desire to help your family is rooted in love. However, it is important that you come to grips with the all-too-common assumption that only by helping are you expressing love. Letting go of the need to help is not letting go of helping. (See Chapter 9 for more on letting go.) You also aid your children by listening to them attentively, by inquiring about their needs, by setting boundaries between you and them and by discussing these boundaries with them. When these acts are infused with love you are less likely to feel pressured into giving them everything they ask for.

Be straightforward. If a problem arises, ask, "How can I help?" or "Is there anything I can do to help?" This does not commit you to financial support; you can still say, "No." But it lays the issue on the table and precludes manipulation. Furthermore, you are making yourself a model as a straight-shooter and a caring parent. If your adult child declines your help, respect her "No."

Be clear about the nature of your financial help. When you set boundaries, both parties feel their wishes are being respected. If you give money, for example, do you consider it a gift or a loan? How do you expect the loan to be repaid? Is the money earmarked for a specific purpose or is it open ended? You need to be clear. There is nothing wrong with saying, for example, "This money is to buy yourself the used piano that you've been wanting."

It is also crucial that in giving or helping you don't have a hidden agenda regarding what will be given in return. Of course, we all want appreciation and signs of recognition, such as more time spent together. However, these expectations, if hidden, will inevitably backfire, producing tension and resentment. Work toward the goal of helping when it feels right and don't expect anything in return.

Give yourself time to make a decision. Talk it through thoroughly with your spouse, partner, or a close friend. You want to feel comfortable with a decision to give or not to give. Making a wise decision also means listening carefully to your adult child's description of her financial situation and her arguments for a gift or loan. Get used to saying, "I'll think about it." And then think about it.

Be aware of any guilt or resentment you are feeling. Guilt and resentment are part of the total picture and usually have a role to play in a big, familial money transaction. If you feel free from them you can consider yourself blessed. Keeping in close touch with any negative feelings you may be having will help you to get these feelings out — ideally, to your son or daughter. You may find yourself saying, for example, "The last time I gave you money it went to pay your credit card bill for your spa vacation. We agreed that it would be a short-term loan, but I've had no repayment for six months. I'm feeling resentful that you are asking me for more."

Your adult child may be adept at manipulation. It is wise to be aware of his techniques, designed to make you feel guilty if you don't accede to his wishes. Here are a few of them:

- You do more for the other children than you do for me.
- You have so much and I have so little.
- You are making it impossible for me to fulfill my dreams.

If you say No to a request, don't let the pendulum swing all the way in the other direction simply on principle. Promiscuous givers, when they experience a revelation about the destructive side of their unrestrained giving, may become rigid non-givers. There is no substitute for looking at each request on its own merits. Continue to be helpful, caring, and loving.

Consider "tough love." If you feel unattended to, exploited by, or deeply resentful toward your adult child, a tough love approach may be appropriate in a given instance. Your child's behavior toward you, which may include neglect, is unacceptable in the light of his request for money or other support. Tough love, essentially, is letting your adult child sink or swim. Don't go down this road unless you can stick to it. Your child may be seeing you in this new guise for the first time. He may not believe you are serious and may try repeatedly to press your vulnerability buttons.

Tough love works best if you can believe in it — guilt free — as the best solution for him, for you, and for your relationship. It may be necessary to adopt a tough love strategy because of your long term unwillingness to set clear boundaries with your adult children. But it is also important to know that it is a last resort.

If your child asks you for financial support, you have a right to know key things about her economic situation. Does your child squander money? Does she use drugs? If you help her out will you merely be supporting her habit? Does your child work? Does she fail to hold on to jobs for more than a short period? If so, why? And finally, does a mental or physical disability make your adult child incapable of self-support? Disabilities may be looked upon by disabled people differently, depending on their commitment to independent living. A severe disability, such as inability to manipulate hands and legs due to cerebral palsy, may make your support decisions easier. A borderline disability, such as dyslexia, may put you on the spot. You suspect that your 25-year-old son's inability to hold on to a job has to do with his dyslexia, but you don't know what to do about it. Can you really let him sink or swim? Can you tolerate your dyslexic child becoming homeless? To make the best decision, you must face your feelings around your child's future without your support.

Be aware that a desire to help an adult child may be masking a desire to be needed, or its first cousin, the sense that you are not doing enough for your children. If your adult child senses that your financial support has strings attached she may reject it, making life unnecessarily difficult for herself and causing you dismay. Your giving has to be for her sake and not for yourself, even if, paradoxically, more giving would give you more pleasure.

Finally, can you afford a gift or a loan to your adult child? If your own finances warrant a No, say so. It is not immoral to be poor, temporarily or otherwise. Let your child know that you love him and will do whatever else you can to help. But do not claim poverty when this is not the case. Your child is likely to know when the claim is phony, and new layers of resentment and alienation will set in. You can say No to a request for money with the simplest of explanations, such as, "It doesn't feel right just now." If he asks why, you can say, "I don't know. It just doesn't." You are under no obligation to give an explanation for your decision, although you may feel that you owe him one. As long as you are not hostile or verbally abusive, a simple response such as the one above may be the best.

Once again, the reason we support our adult children is love. We don't have to, legally, and the moral imperative, as well, is open to question. If we keep love firmly in the forefront of our deliberations, our decisions will almost surely be sound.

Living in the Parental Home

Sharon, a widow of 62, owned a comfortable, three-bedroom home in a picturesque college town on the West Coast. Her oldest daughter,

Ruth Ann, had settled in Israel and married an Israeli. They had recently come to the U.S. to enable Ari to pursue a career in electrical engineering. The couple had settled into Sharon's home for approximately six months, or until Ari was on his feet with a job in his field. Sharon explained the situation this way:

"Somehow it all works. We don't eat together, or at least we do our own food shopping and assume that meals will be separate. You see, they come home from work and school at all hours, and planning formal meals would be too chaotic. Once in a while we get together for a meal but we don't count on it. We didn't get together and establish a bunch of rules before they moved in. We kind of make it up as we go along. That method works for us."

I was in Sharon's home in the late afternoon when her daughter and son-in-law arrived home from work. An easy, relaxed camaraderie prevailed. Ruth Ann and Ari shared their plans for a short trip while Sharon fed the family cat. Ari asked his mother-in-law about the whereabouts of a household tool that he needed, and they spent a bit of time searching for it together. The young couple were at home in Sharon's house; it was their house too, for the time being. There was no sense of trespass or of being beholden. Mother, daughter, and son-in-law shared the same rights and privileges.

It is not always this way. The Carter family, mother and father in their early 30s and two children, 11 and 8, found themselves without a place to live. Jerry Carter, a foreman in an auto plant and his wife, Dee, a homemaker, lost their rented house when the owner decided to live in it. Though Jerry made a decent living, recent dental expenses and the purchase of a much needed car had strained their savings to the limit. They didn't have enough money for a down payment on a house or even for the first-and-last-month's rent on a three-bedroom apartment. Dee's parents, Mary and Jim, who owned a three-bedroom home nearby saw no alternative but to take the whole family in.

The two families never sat down and talked about deadlines, about division of labor or about money. Mary, the matriarch in her home, now made meals for six people every night. Her daughter helped, but long-standing, competitive friction between mother and daughter made this a problem for both of them. Mary complained to her close friends and neighbors about the undisciplined grandchildren and about her increased work load. Her husband Jim had less and less tolerance for his lack of privacy, lost his temper with his wife, and stayed out of the house several nights a week.

Although Jim suggested from time to time that they try to find another solution to their children's housing problem, Mary's bottom line was that she didn't want her grandchildren to be homeless. Moreover, she was afraid to confront her daughter and son-in-law with restrictions or other negative comments for fear of losing her children. Lastly, she felt anxious and unsettled about bringing up never-resolved problems between her daughter and herself. Home life was madcap at best, but a more accurate term would be dysfunctional. The entire family was learning that sharing living space is extremely difficult, even — or especially — with one's children.

Should one collect rent from one's adult child? A sensible answer can only be found if all the relevant variables are looked at. If the parents normally rent the space, they are losing income by not charging rent. If the adult child is temporarily without funds, the decision to house him means not collecting rent, at least for a while. But not collecting any rent, if the adult child can afford some, places her in a seriously dependent position and the parents in a position of control. Collecting rent, however, adds a landlord/tenant component to the already complex parent/child relationship, substituting business values for familial ones. Some adult children fervently want their moms to be mom-like and their dads to be dad-like, not businesslike, check-collecting landlords. But some appreciate and prefer the clarity of spelled-out boundaries and written monetary arrangements. When a business relationship — renting space in one's home to one's children — overlays a familial one, it doesn't mean that business takes precedence over family. On the contrary, the business relationship is in place to preserve loving, family interaction so that resentment and anger don't threaten it.

What can we learn from Sharon's family's experience and from that of the Carter family?

Family members need to communicate, especially when they are in the same living space. Eric Maisel puts it this way:

Any family can do a better job of communicating and living well together. Sometimes this takes major changes, but more often it just takes practicing simple skills and paying better attention to what people in the family are thinking and feeling. Usually, if even one person in the family sets out to improve family communication, the whole family is encouraged and more loving communication can begin.[1]

If you do not say that you would appreciate more quiet before 8 a.m., no one will know this. You might think that they should know it automatically, because in your view, early morning noise-making is inherently inconsiderate. But you don't want to rock the boat and incur anyone's anger; you may want to preserve your image as a generous, flexible, and warm-hearted person. It seems to you that someone, a son or daughter-in-law or grandchild, is forcing you to confront them with criticism or a restraining order, or else to accept the unpleasantness. If you don't put your needs into words, however, resentment is likely to build up and may explode unexpectedly, creating a highly stressful or even violent confrontation.

Setting rules, limits, and deadlines takes the pressure off day-to-day interaction and helps to give scope and structure to the temporary living situation. Sharon's family was able to function effectively without pre-set rules. But they did set a deadline of six months, after which Sharon's daughter and son-in-law would have to move. All parties benefited from having a sense of what the future would look like. The Carter family, on the other hand, muddled along with no rules and hence, with no clear sense of rights and responsibilities. They set no limits, no boundaries, and no deadlines. Mary Carter couldn't imagine her grandchildren being homeless; she therefore gave herself no option but taking them in — indefinitely. It is easy to say that midlife parents should simply not take in their married children and their grandchildren — in this case, a family of four. But life's vicissitudes, especially the high cost of living, make this a very real and common family pattern, particularly among working-class families. For some, the setting of rules and limits feels businesslike, not family-like. But the alternative can be anger, violence, and the loss of the family's ability to heal and nurture.

Over-giving by parents breeds resentment. We are told from early childhood that generosity is a highly valued trait. As toddlers we are admonished to share the favorite toy or delicious cookie. We give birthday and holiday presents and know that our time for getting will come. Yet midlife parents, especially mothers, who take their adult children into their homes sometimes fall into a pattern of promiscuous giving without any thought of reciprocity. They allow their adult children to become dependent on them for shopping, cleaning, and cooking. It is as if they were born to this role; they feel needed beyond their wildest dreams. But they also feel exhausted at the end of the day and, paradoxically, starved for recognition and appreciation. They may express their feelings to friends and neighbors but the behavior pattern and its unexamined motives continues or gets worse. The adult children may exploit their servile parent shamelessly, partly because the parent allows or even encourages them to do so. But the adult children also resent their servile parent; it may be hard for them to respect a mother who is a slave and a dishrag. The situation calls out for insight, intervention, and change of direction. The young Carter family may have to move into its own dwelling, however inadequate, to avoid further, and serious, deterioration of extended-family relations.

Never minimize the importance of spatial boundaries and of privacy. Families all over the world often live in tight quarters. Children do not have the luxury of separate bedrooms (or any bedroom) in most regions of the world. Even in Japan, an advanced, industrial nation, only a very small percentage of the population enjoys spacious living quarters. In Western Europe, the U.S., and Canada, where roomy apartments and three- and four-bedroom homes are commonplace, the issue of privacy takes on new meaning. People are less likely to bump into each other, and the concept of invading one another's space comes into being. We need to recognize the cultural relativity of our definition of privacy.

With larger living spaces come greater expectations. When the four members of the Carter family moved in with their parents, a new perception of comfort (or lack of it) had to be adopted. Jim Carter, especially, had to leave the house several evenings each week. He was finding it hard to breathe in his own home. Cultural relativity notwith-standing, it is always wise to respect the space of others, even if it is only a chair or a bed. Locking oneself in the bathroom is, sadly, one of the ways — sometimes one of the only ways — that people in tight living situations can achieve privacy. When parents take their adult children into their home to live, the privacy issue will always surface. Since it cannot be avoided, parents and their children would do well to face it early and figure out ways to minimize it.

The Competing Needs of Parents and Children

If adult children crave autonomy and their parents are prepared to acknowledge that need for autonomy, the way is clear for mutual understanding and smooth sailing as the adult/adult years progress. Parental needs, however, are sometimes pointed in an altogether different direction from those of their adult children, perpetuating friction, unspoken hurt, and pain. And sometimes it is the parents, not the children, who crave autonomy, as we shall see in the case of Natalie and Erica.

Erica, age 24, had just finished college on the East Coast, and felt she needed a few months respite before she looked for a place to live and a job in journalism, her college major. She asked her mother and stepfather whether she could stay in the family home for a while, until she had a clear sense of what she wanted to do. Erica's mother, Natalie, thought about it for a day and then called Erica with a straightforward response.

"I'm okay with your living here for up to two months. You can have the little room off the kitchen and use the bathroom in the downstairs hall. Dan and I talked about this last night and we both agreed that our privacy is very important to us. We both feel that our wing of the house — the master bedroom, study, and bathroom — should be off limits to you. We feel this is the best way to make it work if you're going to be here for a while."

Erica was taken by surprise. She felt resentment welling up in her; she became sullen and uncommunicative toward Natalie and Dan.

> Then, after about five days, there was a big blow-up.
>
> "What's up?" Natalie asked her daughter as they were preparing a meal. "You seem uncomfortable or angry or something."
>
> "That room you put me in is too small. There's no room for my things. And it's got one small window facing an alley. Why did you put me there?" Erica's voice was rising in pitch, heading toward an emotional explosion. "You've always been like that. I really have a bitch for a mother." After a few more jagged sentences, each one more out of control than the last, Erica dropped a frying pan and ran out of the room.

Natalie was shocked. Over the next few days, she began an obsessive rehashing of the blow-up, the events leading up to it, the exact words Natalie had used when responding, and, most of all, a catalogue of ways she, Natalie, could have prevented it or dealt with it more wisely. Eventually, Natalie came to realize that decades of parental guilt kept her from dealing with the blow-up the way she should have. She imagined conversations with her daughter:

"You are a guest in my house," she said to herself. That sounded right. "You have to treat me decently." That came to the surface with emotion. "I know you have been depressed on and off over the last five or six years. I know you have taken hard drugs. I know some of that was a result of our relationship. But I've already apologized to you for past mistakes — quite a few times. I don't have to keep apologizing, do I?"

Then Natalie hit upon something really new. "I'm sorry I didn't assume you were an adult," she uttered out loud to her imaginary daughter. "I guess I let you lose your temper and yell at me, out of old, unresolved guilt, instead of setting boundaries and feeling okay about them. I didn't trust that you could be a grownup, so I let you say outrageous things to my face, violent things, which I would not have tolerated in anyone else. I felt your violence was my fault."

Once Natalie came face to face with her guilt she was able to make a calm assessment of the reasons for Erica's anger. She put herself in her daughter's place and became aware of the emotional fallout of being told, "You can't come into mom's (and stepfather's) bedroom. It is off limits, out of bounds, not available to you any more." She, Natalie, could have broached the subject with a greater understanding, recognizing that Erica might experience it as rejection or even abandonment. This recognition brought empathy and compassion to her dealings with her daughter, and opened up new and fruitful channels of communication.

Sociologists draw a distinction between primary and secondary relationships.[2] A primary relationship is close, face-to-face, usually long standing, wide-ranging, and intimate. A secondary relationship is practical, usually short term, limited in scope, and non-intimate. The paradigm of a primary relationship is the family. The paradigm of a secondary relationship is business (for example, one's contacts with the bank teller, the grocer, or the barber).

Both types of relationship are part of our lives. In our secondary relationships, our responses tend to be conventional, brief, and more or less superficial. To our casual acquaintances and business contacts we use "please" and "thank you" ; we say, "Have a nice day," or "Enjoy your trip." In our primary relations we sometimes avoid the conventional niceties. It is as though we are trying to recapitulate the time of infancy and early childhood when little ones were altogether dependent and parents were altogether needed. This period, idealized in our memories, was a time before conventional speech kept us civilized — and made us aware that we were slightly apart.

There are those who are deeply drawn to the idealized, familial, primary relationship and, perhaps unwittingly, try to turn all relationships into primary ones. If the person is an adult child, he may want to preserve or recreate the unquestioned acceptance of early childhood: "My parents will never reject me." If the person is the parent of an adult child, she may try to preserve or recreate her young child's dependence: "My child will never leave me."

My daughter has lived outside the family home for about twelve years now. I've noticed that each time she comes to visit she pokes her head into the refrigerator and sniffs around the stove for anything interesting that may be cooking there. Without a by-your-leave she will try a meatball, then a second, maybe a third. She never asks, "Mom, is it all right if I try one of your meatballs?" She just takes them. Children, even adult children, are allowed to do this, she seems to be implying; it's part of family closeness, family togetherness.

It's the primary relationship writ large — and parents are supposed to go along. She reminds me of when she was a little kid; the scene feels like long ago. I think of my own growing-up years and the way my mother and, especially, my grandmother made food-giving into a high art. Nothing gave them more gratification than seeing me eat their offerings, whether they were from the refrigerator, from a pot on the stove, or at the table. They took it as a validation of their parental and grandparental roles when they saw me eat with gusto.

I don't entirely go along with my daughter's recapitulation of this scene. A new model may be called for, a model that deals with the fact that Betsy is an adult and that the mommy/baby separation happened long ago. This new model may be adopted equally by parents and children, for both are prone to the warm and cozy parent/baby model that once gave them so much pleasure.

Ask yourself if you are trying to rebuild or maintain a mommy/little kid or a daddy/little kid relationship. It may be hard to grasp this quality in yourself and to see it clearly. Once you suspect it, you may find it hard to take a close look without faltering. All adults want to see themselves as acting in a grownup fashion. They don't want to imagine themselves as resorting to babyish ways or even mommy-ish or daddy-ish ways to achieve their goals. Yet many parents and adult children avoid some of the basics of adult interpersonal behavior — the use of please and thank you, for example, which seems to go with secondary relationships. We mouth these words freely with the grocer, the TV repair person, the mail delivery person, or a neighbor up the street. Did we say please to our two-year-old when asking for something at the dinner table? It's hard to remember. Maybe we did some of the time. Maybe we also said, "Give the spoon to daddy," or the like. It seemed okay at the time. We were not brimming with formalities. It was, after all, a primary relationship.

If we discover, as we look inward and backward, that we loved the closeness and informality of the time when our children were little, we may also discover that we want to perpetuate those qualities. Your child may be 29 or 34 or 41 but he may want, nevertheless, to be free to take three meatballs out of your cooking pot without asking or saying "please." You may be thinking, "He's my child, surely he's free to eat whatever he wants when he's in my house; if I make demands or ask for formal politeness he will recoil, give me dirty looks, not understand, move apart, not talk. It's okay. It's his home too, kind of. He's my son. He's not just anyone. And I love him."

Establishing Civility

Establishing and maintaining an adult/adult relationship with your adult child requires that you adopt some of the interpersonal strategies of secondary relationships.

Putting some social distance between us and them is just as potent a tool for adult children as it is for their parents. There are at least three reasons why this is so:

- By saying please and thank you in all situations in which the words are appropriate, the adult child is modeling social distance for the parent who may be overly involved. The parent may not, at first, accept the please or thank you graciously. Some parents may say, "Oh, don't be ridiculous," when their adult child thanks them for a gift. This conveys the message that it is normal and natural for a parent to give her child gifts, and doesn't require a thank you. This message is destructive of healthy interaction because of the unspoken assumption. A thank you is an acknowledgment by the receiver that the gift was freely given. But the over-involved parent doesn't want to acknowledge this choice. She feels that she had to give it, that it was a natural outgrowth of the parent/child connection — as natural as walking and talking. How could she not give to her beloved child?

Similarly, the parent may model social distance for his son or daughter, by regularly using please and thank you with his

> *Establishing and maintaining an adult/adult relationship with your adult child requires that you adopt some of the interpersonal strategies of secondary relationships.*

adult child. The message here is this: We two may have a close, warm, familial bond, but we still have to deal with each other on many practical, non-intimate levels, such as, "Please pass the salt." "Pass the salt, Pop," may feel friendly and familial, but it may also rankle.

- If the adult child declines often enough to say thank you and use other expressions of civility, the parent (who has limits, after all) may begin to feel put upon. Allowing the adult child to adopt the role of the irresponsible baby or young child has a serious down side for the midlife parent, as we saw in the case of the Carter family. The parent may feel ambivalent, wanting to be the indispensable caregiver but, at the same time, needing his space and his time for R and R, and wishing to keep his limited financial resources.

  In a similar vein, an adult child may get fed up with a parent who repeatedly avoids gestures of civility and adopts an expressive style that lacks the controls of secondary relationships. The parent may behave in ways she believes are warm and friendly but which come across to her adult child as pushy and invasive.

- In general, please, thank you, you're welcome, don't mention it, and similar conventions are powerful tools of civility and reciprocity. Their capacity for keeping all relationships healthy cannot be overestimated. They are never out of place, whether in the bed chamber or in international negotiations. By no means do they define all of human intercourse but they go a long way towards making clear the network of interdependent roles that characterizes all of human life.

In sum, either the parent or the adult child may wish for a primary relationship that is modeled after the all-giving parent and the all-taking baby. In order for an adult/adult relationship to develop, each party has to employ distancing mechanisms, one of which is saying thank you. He is borrowing tools from secondary relationships to establish civility.

I have devoted some extended space to the issue of civility because it often goes unnoticed, or at least unlabeled. It burrows into dark corners of our consciousness and often doesn't see the light of day as an issue that calls for discussion, sharing of feelings, or changing of behavior by one or both parties. Other competing needs of parents and adult children need to be addressed, and the table below spells out some of the more vexing.

Finally, parents and adult children may be in competition for the same things: acknowledgment, recognition, appreciation, and love. But they may be wary of giving these to each other for fear that there is a limited quantity of these scarce and precious resources: if they give them away, there will be none left for themselves. This balance scale or zero-sum mentality can exist between spouses, siblings, and friends. Wherever it is found, it is toxic. Finding out for yourself that love

Parents	Adult Children
• may want adult children to feel obligated in order to hold on to them.	• don't want to feel obligated.
• want recognition for all they've done for their children.	• want acknowledgment for their own achievements.
• may want acknowledgment of their experience.	• don't want to be demeaned for lack of experience.
• if newly single, may be looking for or may have already found a new mate.	• may not want to see their parent as sexually active, which they may feel is a role reserved for the young.
• may be embarking on new projects (career, travel, sports) which make them unavailable to their adult children.	• may want more quality time with their parents or may want their parents to spend more time with grandchildren.
• may now have the time and money to be really involved in their kid's activities.	• may want parents out of the picture in order to find their own way.

breeds love, that there is enough to go around, and that when you give recognition to another, that person is moved to recognize you is a discovery of lofty proportions that will enrich your relations with your adult children till the end of your days.

The challenges for parents:

- to make the goal of independence for your adult child a guide to all your actions.
- to give financial support to your adult child for his benefit, not for yours.
- to set boundaries, rules, limits, and deadlines where appropriate.
- to become aware of your feelings of guilt, resentment, or manipulation
- to respect family members' privacy.
- to communicate your preferences for "house rules" to those living in your home, rather than expecting your adult child to know them.
- not to give promiscuously to your adult child.
- to use please, thank you, and similar conventions of civility.
- to recognize that both you and your adult children ultimately want the same things — acknowledgment, recognition, appreciation, and love — and that there is enough for both of you.

8
___

GRANDPARENTING

A Fresh Look for the New Millennium

When the old men gather, they say:
"When I was a boy!"
It really is the land of nowadays that we
never discover. — Booth Tarkington

GRANDCHILDREN ARE A very special legacy of parenthood, one which many parents look forward to with great anticipation as they approach their middle years. With grandchildren, the pressure is off; one doesn't have to produce and socialize a healthy, responsible, well-functioning person. That is now the job of your son or your daughter and their partners. But you aren't just anybody; the kin connection can be a powerful one. You have a role to play, but one which is different, in some ways, from the role of your grandparents.

In spite of good intentions, grandparents and their grandchildren don't always connect. You want to have a storybook relationship with your grandchildren but you may bridle at the way your son or daughter is bringing them up. Your grandchildren may find you too rigid or uncompromising, your home not a familiar, child-centered one. Or you may have the reverse experience: Your children may be more perfectionist and demanding with their children than you think is wise. You want to play a meaningful role but, as is often the case, you may be separated from them by a hundred or a thousand miles, kept from seeing them by busy and complicated schedules.

The desirability of grandchildren — especially the feeling that through them your line will continue — comes up against a new

152

attitude, that of refraining from contributing to population increase. As I alluded to briefly in Chapter 5, the diminishing need to have children (and, by extension, grandchildren) is very recent and still not fully assimilated into the culture as a whole. We do know that many would-be grandparents will have to reconsider their roles in the second half of life.

The New Grandparent

How is the grandparent of today different from the grandparent of 50 years ago? Social institutions of all sorts have been affected by the Big Bang described in Chapter 1. Grandparenting is no exception: the new grandparent is a product of the changing economic landscape. Authors Zalman Schachter-Shalomi and Ronald S. Miller explain the change this way:

> *the model for mentoring clearly comes from the multi-generational family. Throughout history, a natural transmission of values took place from grandparents to grand-children when the family lived under one roof. Living in close proximity to grandchildren, elders educated them in essential values, carried on religious traditions, and made history meaningful by preserving a living link to the past. Today, however, because the traditional family has splintered into the nuclear family and in many cases the single-parent family, we are losing the natural transmission that used to take place intergenerationally.[1]*

Let us look more closely at the ways in which this breakdown of the traditional — or extended — family has affected the institution of grandparenthood. The nuclear family, which began to come into its own following World War II in industrial countries, has left the extended family configuration far behind. Cars, highways, and, of course, suburbs, helped this to happen. Homes and apartments are not big enough to house grandparents, not to mention collateral relatives. Yet, fifty years ago my husband's grandparents lived in a rambling, Bronx apartment — many small rooms off a long hall — that also housed their widowed second daughter and her two small children. It was home, as well, to their third and fourth daughters when they were in their twenties and thirties. Just as midlife families took in their elderly parents, they also took in their grown children and their grandchildren when they had nowhere else to go. Today's grandparent, however, may not be taken into the home of her grown children. She may find herself facing one of several current options: a retirement home, a small apartment near one of the children, or simply staying where she has always lived.

Grandparents are no longer matriarchs or patriarchs. Their advice is requested infrequently, and may be ignored. Their memories of the flapper era, the Great Depression, World War II, or of their forced exodus from Europe during the 1940s are not generally treasured by their children and grandchildren who can now learn about such highlights of history from the Internet. Their age and experience, sadly, mean little in an age when a computer is deemed out of date after a few years.

Grandparents of today may feel unclear about their role. They remember their own grandpa and grandma as integral to their family, either living in the family home or visiting often. They remember being taken on small excursions by their grandparents, being given special treats and having grandma or grandpa all to themselves, sometimes for long periods. Grandma and grandpa were not shy about giving advice or about actively participating in family life. Their authority may have been kept at bay by their adult children but there were many points at which they were able to connect with their grandchildren. Visiting with them was a given, not a choice.

The 21st century grandparent, on the other hand, may be a stranger to his grandkids. And if that grandparent is widowed or divorced, the problem is compounded. He or she may have to travel some distance to see them, often a long solitary drive, and may have to settle for seeing them once a month or even less frequently.

Unlike fifty years ago, both parents — and many midlife grandparents — work. Family scheduling can be very complicated, with everyone leaving in the early morning, often at different times, to arrive more or less on time at jobs, school, or childcare. Family life often doesn't begin again until 7 p.m. or later. How does this affect grandparents? Because their time with their children is so limited, parents do not necessarily want to share it with grandparents on the weekends.

Because of this lack of clarity about the grandparents' role and because of their loss of authority, today's grandparent may be very wary about criticizing his children's child-rearing practices. Several of my interviewees said that they never criticize their children in this sphere, and added comments such as, "It's their life," or, "We've had our turn; now it's theirs." Although this sounds prudent and wise, it may, unfortunately, mask a loss of connection. Not all interventions by grandparents of fifty or one hundred years ago were necessarily bossy, impertinent, or unwanted by their children. Although family members got into each other's hair, especially if they lived together in close quarters, grandparents could contribute to some decision-making around child-rearing, if only by being with their grandchildren on a regular basis.

Because their time with their children is so limited, parents do not necessarily want to share it with grandparents on the weekends.

This brings us to a final item on a short but, I think, provocative list of changes in the institution of grandparenthood: baby-sitting. The busy family of today with two working parents, has, it seems, a bottomless-pit need for baby-sitting services. Although working parents may want to be with their kids on the weekends, there is an equally strong pull toward an all-adult evening out or short vacation. If grandma comes over to visit, their children will often want to take advantage of her visit by getting away. Parents may not have been to the movies together for many months. Their expenses for regular childcare during the working day make them think twice about spending more on the weekends. They may feel guilty about going out without the children — but leaving them with grandma may relieve that guilt. Baby sitting, however, is not quite the same thing for grandma and grandpa as visiting the grandchildren and spending some good-quality time with them: it has an obligatory ring to it that is hard to dismiss. One of my respondents went to a distant city to baby-sit for her grandchildren for one week while her daughter and son-in-law vacationed. She felt some resentment but was also somewhat flattered: she was, after all, being trusted with the precious cargo. But she would much rather have been asked, "Mom, come and visit. We'd love to see you."

Amy, a 65-year-old widowed grandmother, lived about fifty miles from her daughter and son-in-law and their two children, aged five and nine. She carried with her an image of grandparenthood that included many warm and fuzzy things. The grandchildren would be delighted to see their grandmother and would greet her with open arms. They would be happy to go on trips and outings with her. They would thank her spontaneously for gifts and treats. They would think of her as a "special" person and their relationship would be special as well. They would respect her authority when their parents were not present. Amy didn't stop to think of the many preconceptions that were part of her vision of grandparenthood: she was unaware that she was idealizing the role. But as time progressed it became clear that her experience and her preconceived image of the role of grandparent were very far apart.

The difference between what Amy wanted and what she was getting dawned upon her when her granddaughter, then three, declined to greet her with a hug, or even with a smile. Amy, who saw her grandchildren about once a month, countered little Amelia's shyness with a great deal of attention and display of affection, but to no avail. Amelia wanted her Mommy, and treated Grandmother Amy as a stranger, or worse, an interloper. Amy's daughter, Denise, tried to smooth things over by saying to her recalcitrant daughter, "Give Grandma Amy a hug." Of course, it didn't work; it rarely does. The hug was perfunctory and satisfied neither granddaughter nor grandmother.

Amy tried not to take her grandchildren's lack of enthusiasm personally. She did, however, ask herself what she could do differently. She didn't quite know if she was doing anything wrong, or if there was something lacking in her grandmotherly commitment. One thing she was sure of, however. She was not about to criticize her daughter and son-in-law or say anything negative about their children's relationship with her. She would just plow along trying (and pretending) to be an ideal grandparent.

Then, one day, Amy made what amounted to a breakthrough. She found the words — and the unthreatening tone — with which to broach the topic of the children's apparent lack of affection for her. She put it in universal rather than personal terms, something like the following: "You know, sometimes it's hard for parents to know what to do when their kids don't act towards relatives and friends the way they would like them to — like when they fail to say hello or good-bye or please or thank you. And in some families they don't see grandparents very often so they don't get to build up a solid relationship with them."

Denise picked up on the theme and allowed a rich and fruitful discussion to ensue. Amy was thrilled because she knew that the door to honest communication with her daughter had been opened. She sensed that Denise was relieved of the burden of trying to cover up awkward interaction. She came to understand more fully that her granddaughter was shy with others and that her grandson, the older of the two, was preoccupied with sports. Grandma was not being singled out for rejection. Denise helped her to understand the kinds of child-ish play that would help to reduce Amelia's self-consciousness. Grandma Amy came to understand that it is possible to discuss delicate subjects with one's children concerning grandparenthood if one does so with love, not criticism, as one's guide.

Grandparents as Alternative Role Models for their Grandchildren

Despite the ongoing dissolution of the extended family, grandparents are not merely a useless appendage in the lives of their grandchildren. Their roles are more tentative and tenuous than in their parents' and grandparents' generation but they have not disappeared altogether. The challenge is to understand the limitations of the role and to exert loving care and influence in the lives of one's grandchildren without undermining their parents' authority.

With this challenge in mind, it may be the right moment to re-examine, once again, some of the principles of communication outlined in Chapter 2. Strategies such as active listening, using I-statements, not interrupting, and not overtalking are useful and productive in all interactions, but they are particularly cogent when dealing with young grandchildren.

Parents of young children are deeply immersed in the primary functions of molding, socializing, character-building, and protecting their children from harm. Grandparents, when alone with their grandchildren, can take a rest from some of these primary parent functions. Moreover, when their visits are a month or more apart, they may not be aware of some of the fine point of the parents' child-rearing practices. However, grandparents have a fine and positive role to play using active listening. Small children love to be listened to; they are perfecting their spoken language skills and greatly enjoy putting new experiences into words. Parents, with the best of intentions, may be unwilling to take the time to just listen — so many daily pressures intervene. The helping professions, from the "talking cure" — psychoanalysis — to job counseling, derive much of their power and usefulness from active listening. It has been suggested more than once that just being listened to accounts for a large part of the success of any counseling program. Grandparents can become inspired listeners for each of their grandchildren, thereby building a special bond between them. And here is a bonus: Listening to little children's stories is easy and fun.

> *Grandparents can become inspired listeners for each of their grandchildren, thereby building a special bond between them. And here is a bonus: Listening to little children's stories is easy and fun.*

Not having true authority over grandchildren, as past generations of grandparents often did, does not mean you have nothing substantial to offer them. You are different from their parents in a variety of ways, and they are intrigued by your differentness. If you live in a big city and they live in a suburb, you can pique their imagination around big city life — subways, tall buildings, parades, street life, ethnic neighborhoods. If you live in the back woods, you can introduce them to vegetable gardening, bird watching, or wild animal habitats. They will remember excursions with you on your home turf for the rest of their lives. Some of their important life choices will be influenced by their grandparents' different lifestyle.

There are some families in which the grandparent has a measure of authority by default. Consider the case of Brenda, a grandmother in her 60s, whose daughter, Vikki, was enmeshed in a marriage that was dysfunctional and whose granddaughter was at risk. Vikki and her husband, John, had recently gone through a court-ordered separation. John, in spite of abusive behavior towards Vikki on nights when he came home drunk, was not yet locked out of his house. He demanded access to his daughter, Gina, and took her on Sunday trips to amusement parks and on drives to far-off places. Vikki was worried about his alcohol level when driving with Gina in addition to his general aggressiveness. He had also smacked Gina across the face a few times. Vikki was scared of her husband and couldn't confront him. John's behavior was unpredictable and family life was unsettled, to say the least.

Brenda baby-sat for her granddaughter, Gina, three days a week, usually for the entire day. Her daughter Vikki had a job as a companion to an elderly woman which was vital for the family's financial survival. Gina was sometimes left with not enough warm clothing, without any toys or games, or with a cold or sore throat that had not been attended to. Brenda understood that she had to take on some of the obligations of a parent. Twice she took Gina to a medical clinic and paid for the visits and the medicine herself. She dealt with other emergencies as well, sometimes without consulting with Vikki. It became clear to her that her judgment was clearer and her priorities were sounder than those of her daughter. She had become a grandparent in loco parentis.

When a grandparent takes on the role of parent he or she will very likely set different rules of conduct or safety for the grandchild. Elizabeth, an African-American grandmother, took on the role of parent for her nine-year-old grandson, Peter, when the boy's mother died. Elizabeth's son worked night-shift and felt he couldn't do a proper job of parenting. Elizabeth knew two other grandmothers from her church who were raising grandchildren; the role was not unknown in her community. Nevertheless, it changed her life dramatically and also gave her a deep sense of usefulness.

Elizabeth set fairly strict limits and boundaries for Peter, an active and sports-loving child, who would, she knew, soon be an even more active adolescent. She insisted that he come straight home from school each day, that he always tell her where he was going, and that he do his homework before going out to play. Peter's grandmother's home had more structure than his parents' home had had. Elizabeth was in a position, furthermore, to make decisions about Peter's upbringing without continually checking with her son, Rob. The trust which Rob had in his mother's judgment allowed all parties to benefit.

Yet Elizabeth understood that she wasn't the child's parent, and that she had to tread lightly at times. She knew that Peter could visit his father's home at any time, a home that had little structure but lots of easy living and good times. Her child-rearing style as a grandmother had to be modified by Rob's existence as a male role-model in Peter's life.

Clichés Around the Role of Grandparent

It is easy to be seduced into believing some of the clichés about grandparenthood — that it is a wonderful role which you have earned, and that you therefore fully deserve all the gratifying perks that it brings. Another well-worn set of clichés revolves around ways in which your grandchildren resemble their parents — in looks, habits, and personality. You and your adult children may share fantasies about your grandchildren's future success, say, in med school or on the stage. It is best to be aware of the lure of clichés and to avoid them as much as possible.

Coming into grandparenthood with the "wonderful role" image firmly planted in your head may set you up for disappointment. It did just that for Janice and Elliot, both agnostic Jews with strong humanistic values and a belief in public service. Their son, David, was a member of the Woodstock generation. David didn't work, exactly, and his parents suspected that he survived on proceeds from drug dealing. They did their best to accept his long hair and unpredictable outfits. In his early 20s, he lived with a young woman in a one-room flat in a youth-culture neighborhood of a big city. To everyone's surprise, the couple got married, and spent the next two years following charismatic rock bands around the country. David's parents' liberal and tolerant belief systems and hopes for their son were being pushed to the limit.

After three years the marriage broke up. David did some soul-searching and decided to try to finish college. It was there that he met and fell in love with Rachel, also a reformed flower child who came from a secular Jewish home. David and Rachel set their wedding date a year hence. In the meantime, they learned everything they could about Orthodox Judaism and decided to follow that religious path. This was a turnabout that Janice and Elliot were not prepared for. But more surprises were in store when grandchildren appeared.

David's parents loved him and were proud of his decision to finish college and prepare himself for a good career. They no longer worried that he might be picked up for vagrancy or, worse yet, die from an overdose. They approached the coming of their first grandchild with great anticipation and joy.

Shortly after a healthy, baby girl was born, David, his wife and child moved 400 miles away to a city that had many religious and educational opportunities for Orthodox Jewish families. Janice and Elliot were able to visit them only about once every three months. They weren't present at their granddaughter's first birthday, and they also missed the birth of their first grandson, six months later. Eventually, five children were born, one of them with Down's syndrome.

Janice and Elliot were frustrated because their own work obligations prevented them from participating more in their grandchildren's lives. Janice, especially, felt called to give mountains of love and attention to her little grandson with Down's syndrome. She and Elliot both wanted to be helpful to their son's big, bustling family, but it wasn't to be. For one thing, Jewish dietary laws made it almost impossible to take the children out for restaurant meals or to buy them snacks at the circus or a baseball game. The grandparents' non-kosher kitchen made it impossible for David and his family to stay at their home when they came to visit. Janice and Elliot began to resent the religious laws and restrictions that that made it more difficult for them to be the ideal grandparents that they dreamed of being.

Janice and Elliot experienced approximately twelve years of part-time, very restricted grandparenting. At first they felt that the wonderful role of grandparenting was being denied them and they struggled with what they perceived as a loss. But gradually they came to see their situation differently. They began to realize, first of all, that their son and daughter-in-law had picked themselves up from the non-achieving, risky, street world of the '70s to become educated, self-supporting, solid citizens. Their children's religious path was a conduit for strong moral and familial values, which were sometimes, but not always, different from their own. Furthermore, it could not be denied that David and Rachel were good parents. The children were loved, attended to, and amazingly independent.

Janice and Elliot came to understand that, although they were not greatly needed as grandparents for help and advice, they were still loved and appreciated and greeted warmly whenever they visited. They knew, also, that their five beautiful grandchildren were the strong individuals that they were partly because of them — their stability, their values, and their love.

I asked Janice whether she ever offered advice to David and Rachel about child rearing.

"Only when they ask me," she responded.

"When have they asked you for advice?" I continued.

"I can't actually remember a single time," she answered.

Not only do Janice and Elliot not give advice, they also proclaim that every decision that their children make is wonderful. They prefer not to test the fragility of their relationship by trying to fine-tune the family's choices, especially around child-rearing. Their son and his family have a good life but it is very different from their own. The strategy that works for them is not to criticize anything that their children and grandchildren do.

The cliché that one's grandchild is sure to be a chip off the old block hits a wall when he doesn't satisfy the expected image. A muscular, athletic dad produces a thin, slight son, perhaps fearful of contact sports; a musical, violin-playing mother produces a tone-deaf daughter who wants to get married and have a family — period. Further, adopted children are chips off of some other old block. The desire to see a positive and recognizable family trait carried on in the next generations can sometimes be as strong in grandparents as in parents, perhaps stronger. Grandparents would do well to face up to their fantasies concerning their grandchildren's future, fame and fortune.

How a Sound Relationship with Grandchildren Impacts the Relationship with Your Adult Children

Just as having children doesn't necessarily strengthen a marriage, the appearance of grandchildren doesn't necessarily improve relations between you and your adult children. But it can. Your children want you to love their children. Their children are a gift to you.

There is a palpable quid pro quo here: After all you have done for your kids, raising them to functioning adulthood, they are repaying you with a unique and precious gift that only they can give you. You are being asked to honor this intergenerational gift with the awe that human procreation inspires. You are now part of the ongoing stream of humanity. Without you, this little person would not have been born (or, if adopted, would not have grown to adulthood having absorbed your family's unique qualities).

The weakening of extended family does not mean the loss of kin connection. Grandparents are a category apart from all others. Their specialness extends beyond genes or "family line." Grandparents bond with their newly adopted grandson from Korea or their six-month-old granddaughter of Filipino/African heritage in a matter of days, if not hours. More often than not they are spilling over with anticipation and excitement towards this amazing new family member. They wear their new grandparent status with pride because they know that, at some level, the new baby is theirs as well as their children's.

Knowing that you love their children and will go to bat for them can be very healing to the parent/adult child relationship. You and they now have something incontrovertible in common: love and caring for a tiny person in your midst. Young adult parents are easily seduced into dropping their animosities toward their parents when they see the glow of happiness and pride in their parents' eyes as they bond with their grandchildren. Lifetime interpersonal problems don't disappear overnight, but they can mellow. Parents and their adult children who claim to have nothing in common now have a new family member who needs their love and nurturing. One could say that grandparents don't have to do anything; they just need to be there, bonding with new kin and being links in the great chain of being.

But passivity isn't for everyone; many prefer to take an active and creative role whenever possible. Grandparents are well advised to do things with their grandchildren that parents can't or won't do. Youngsters will remember that wonderful trip to the Hopi reservation, to New York City, or to a Red Sox double-header as something great they did with grandma and grandpa. Such special excursions without parents give grandparents and grandchildren a chance to get to know each other and to allow grandparents to be fully in authority for a short span of time.

Grandparents' exercise of authority and their rules of decorum and safety will be somewhat different from those of the parents. Grandparents have the challenging task of figuring out how far they want to go in directions that may be different from the parents' child-rearing prescriptions and proscriptions. A trip away from home may be the only time grandparents are seen by their grandchildren as authority figures. Grandparents have an opportunity to demand respect from grandchildren who may never have been taught to treat them with respect.

Treating grandchildren to an adventurous outing can give working parents a rest from parenting, a time for R and R. In the best of all worlds the grandparents won't feel that the grandchildren are being dumped on them in order that the parents can have a vacation. The parents, similarly, won't feel a lack of trust, a sense that the grandparents are not on the same child-rearing wavelength as they are. One of my respondents, an enthusiastic, actively participating grandmother, bristled when her daughter called her to task for saying to her granddaughter, "Be a big girl." Of course, grandma meant well, as grandparents usually do. But the message was very clear: "Do it our way. We are the final authorities and judges of what's best for our child." Suffice it to say, potential conflicts between parents and grandparents over child-rearing strategies should be anticipated and, if possible, worked out in advance.

The Would-be Grandparent

Throughout human history, married couples have been expected to raise a family. In all cultures, marriage or close male/female bonding has been associated with bearing, raising, socializing, and protecting children. Even when couples do not produce a child, it is assumed that they would like to but can't. Only in the last 40 years or so has it become acceptable for married men and women to profess openly that they do not want children. Some take this stand because they do not want to add to the already overpopulated planet. Some don't care for children or do not want to take on the responsibilities of parents.

As a result, a new category has emerged — the would-be grandparent. Parents in their fifties, sixties and seventies find themselves with children, sometimes three or four, but with no promise of grandchildren. For example, they may have one son who is in a homosexual relationship (with no interest in adopting), another son who, with his career-minded wife, has decided against children, and a daughter who has had numerous relationships both gay and straight and is now an unmarried forty-year-old. Would-be grandparents come to understand that getting married and having a family isn't automatic; it may not even be the norm. There may still be some who continue to ask their sons and daughters, "When are you going to get married?" or "When are you going to have children?" But in today's world, we need a different model and a new vision — one that will supplant these questions and the attitudes that underlie them.

All would-be grandparents need to respect the highly personal nature of the decision to have or not to have children. Putting pressure on one's children to reproduce will not have the desired results and may very likely have some negative interpersonal consequences. Even before the new paradigm started becoming a part of our social consciousness, such pressure was tactless at best and could threaten to seriously alienate children from their parents. The bottom line is that would-be grandparents can do nothing about the their adult children's choice not to have children. They would do well, therefore, to find creative ways to bring young children into their lives, such as foster-grandparent programs and elementary school tutoring. They would benefit, also, if they can find in themselves new resources of grace and acceptance.

In today's rapidly changing world, would-be grandparents can find ways to project their individuality into the future by means other than grandchildren. Just as feminism raises our consciousness about arenas in which women can participate and excel — such as politics, the professions, the arts. and sports — a new consciousness is emerging regarding the possibilities for creativity, excellence, and new beginnings for people in their sixties and beyond. Midlifers have an ever greater hope of healthy longevity awaiting them. Can they start a new life when their children are grown? Go back to school? Take up a new line of work? Become politically active? Help to heal the planet? It is hoped that many of them can and will.

We have talked about bringing up our children to be independent; we are urged to nurture them sensitively and then let them fly. It is equally important, as we approach the midlife years, to nurture, understand, and develop ourselves — that is to say, to plant the seeds of a healthy independence. These seeds need to be watered, fertilized, and tended. Independence takes effort and courage — and vigilance. To cry into our pillows because our adult children don't give us support or because we don't have loving grandchildren to brighten our days leads us down a blind alley. Each of us then has the task of finding her or his way out. The sunny world of creative options and exciting engagement is out there waiting for our vigorous participation. I have friends and acquaintances — 60-somethings and 70-somethings — who are volunteering as tutors in adult literacy programs, giving workshops on aging, learning how to play a musical instrument or to paint with oils, joining a gym for the first time, and writing humorous pieces for a local newspaper. Whatever turns you on — whatever engages you — is very likely the thing that gets you over the hump. You are no longer a would-be grandparent or a would-be anything else.

The challenge for parents:

- to understand how the breakdown of the extended family is affecting you.
- not to assume that the "wonderful world of grandparenting" will necessarily prevail for you.

- to recognize that loving your grandchildren can begin to heal your damaged relationship with your adult children.
- to be sensitive to the effect of work obligations on your adult children, and the way this impacts their relationship with you — and your grandchildren's relationship with you.
- to think twice before giving your children child-rearing advice.
- to discuss child-sitting issues with your children in a manner that will minimize future conflict.
- to discuss child-rearing issues with your children before taking your grandchildren on a trip or outing.
- to listen attentively to your grandchildren.
- to apply other communication strategies, such as not interrupting, not talking too much, and using I-statements.
- to accept your grandchild as he is, rather than expecting him to be a chip off the old block.
- to develop your own independence and discover meaningful activities that will help you to avoid the pangs of would-be grandparenthood.

9

THE CHALLENGE OF THE FUTURE

*Growing into Mature Relationship
with Your Adult Children*

> If there's no hatred in a mind
> Assault and battery of the wind
> Can never tear the linnet from the leaf.
> — William Butler Yeats

IF YOU ARE A HEALTHY MIDLIFE PARENT, you might very well live to see your children become seniors. You may see your 65-year-old daughter or 68-year-old son have children of their own whose hair is graying. Your great-grandchildren may be about to enter college. What are we to make of these new population statistics? How do they affect the way we interact with our adult children? And what, if anything, needs to be changed?

This book has laid out and examined aspects of midlife parenting, spelling out the challenges and the probable successes that await us if we follow a certain path. This path can be summed up in the phrase "letting go." This much-used catch phrase really does tell us, in a weighty little nutshell, the direction that we need to take. We may have already begun to let go when our children were in their teens, or even earlier — with positive results for them and for us. Letting go is very easy to understand but often very difficult to accomplish.

In this last chapter we will explore just what letting go is all about and what obstacles and hindrances we face when we embark on that path. I have isolated a number of distinct ways of looking at the concept, which includes letting go of long-standing attitudes, followed by discussions of letting go and selfishness, letting go and aging, and finally, letting go as experienced by your adult children. At best, the obstacles to letting go create stagnation in our relationships; at worst, they destroy our wishes for calm, gentle, and loving interaction. Some of these suggestions will already be familiar from previous chapters, in which the theme of letting go has been a persistent, underlying voice. There is some overlap in the categories, as life seldom provides us with clean boundary lines between closely related needs. Our goal is to get to the riches that lie in wait for us at the end of the path.

A Close Look at Letting Go

Letting go of power

Parents automatically have power from day one of their child's life. Parents' lives are permanently changed by this power — which carries with it great responsibility and, as a corollary to this, fear of making mistakes. The stress associated with exercising this responsibility makes some of us (or all of us, some of the time) want to get away from it, take a break, not have to make all of the critical decisions all of the time. Even so, we find it hard to imagine giving up the power that has been thrust upon us.

In fact, no one likes to give up power. It is alluring, beguiling, seductive, bringing with it perks, or so we think. It extends our selves into the world and may help to ward off feelings of isolation and lone-liness and invisibility. Power makes us feel important, useful, significant, even unique. And here in our midst is our child — albeit an adult child — over whom we have had the mandate to exercise power. We have brought him into the world and raised him to adulthood, exercising our power mandate repeatedly to make decisions about his welfare. And, if we're one of the lucky ones, he's a decent human being and a functioning member of society. So why not continue doing what we've always done? After all, we're older than he is, more experienced, and (we think) wiser.

But parents are never quite sure they are using, or have been using, their power correctly. The line between proper and improper exercise of power is fuzzy. Spanking, for example, was traditionally part of a parent's arsenal of child rearing strategies, but it can turn seriously harsh and become a reportable misdemeanor or felony. Insisting that one's child be civil, respectful, and non-violent is also part of a parent's job description. Yet, with a seemingly slight turn of the screw, one can produce a frightened and unhappy "respectful" child. To put it another way, potential abuse of our power can be a threat to our equanimity. Some parents who would be considered child abusers by any standard, deny that they are any such thing. But others worry constantly about the limitations on their mandate to mold, modify, or manipulate their children.

Added to this is the layer of guilt that haunts all parents, that seems impossible to wipe away. Guilt is painful; feelings of guilt may produce unconscious resentment toward the child for causing it. Authoritarian parenting, while it may have strong cultural, historical, or class roots, is also embedded in the desire to alleviate guilt. "Don't argue; just do as I say" is an attempt to cut off the possibilities of discussion and change, not only in the child but in the parent as well. "There is only one right way to do this" denies the possibility that the child may have an equally valid way, or that the parent might have made a serious mistake all these years.

Although the connection may not always be apparent, letting go is a form of relinquishing power. Our power over our children may seem to be a natural and never-ending state of being that parents are heir to, but it is no such thing. Our power as parents is a transitory state, meaningful only when children are more or less helpless. As they gain in autonomy and ability to cope in the world, our power wanes. This is as it should be. Failing to let the process happen naturally, trying to keep our power as it used to be, has dreadful consequences for parents, for their children and for the parent/child relationship.

Authors Carol Flax and Carl Ubell, in their perceptive book *Mother/Father/You*, put it this way: "Parents may want to unlearn their parental role of power and responsibility: of no longer taking personally — if they ever did — their adult child's mistakes... Older parents continue to act toward their adult children as if they still had the responsibility of bringing them up even though the kids grew up decades ago."[1]

Letting go of the need to be in control

The need to be in control may best be seen as subsumed under, or perhaps a variant of, the larger theme of power. We may want to maintain control in a relationship because we find it comfortable to copy the way our parents treated us. If they made perfectionist demands on us, we may repeat their behavior and imitate their style. Sadly, we are often only dimly aware of our self-hatred for not fighting back. Childhood sibling relationships, in which controlling or being controlled played a big part, may also provide us with a model for later behavior. And some parents' need to control seems to grow from a fear of the loss of the child — a fear that the child will grow up, move away, and perhaps, not come back.

Authors Susan Jonas and Marilyn Nissenson, in their book on mothers and adult daughters have this to say about parental control:

> *The paradox — the revelation — has been that by giving up the outmoded wish to control our daughters on some level, we're not losing a connection but actually gaining a stronger one. Achieving an adult friendship with them is much more of an enriching experience than we would have imagined. Our inclination as mothers had often been to concentrate on what was going on in our daughters' lives, because we thought that was the parental way of staying connected. But now we've come to value a greater reciprocity in our relationship with them.[2]*

It is important to recognize that not all parents share this fear. Some, who may never have felt quite comfortable with parenthood, are openly relieved to gain their freedom when the children leave home. Any loss they may feel is balanced by the gain of free time for projects, pleasures, and self-development.

Nevertheless, for many of us the fear of losing the child lurks in the background — or perhaps on the sidelines — of our parenting life from the time our children are babies. We bond with our offspring and our lives are transformed; we re-define our identities — we are now mothers and fathers — and our family life is irrevocably changed. Our sense of carrying our unique qualities into the future, of having a lasting influence on the world through our progeny can be an immensely powerful enhancement of our sense of self.

If our children are lost to us through death or disappearance or cutting off contact, this sense of self may be in jeopardy. Furthermore, fear of losing the child may cause us to suffer insecurity to the extent that we don't really want our children to grow up. Attempting to control and manipulate our adult children can be a way of keeping them dependent and within our grasp, thereby miring them in a child-like state.

As we have seen throughout this book, the need to control our adult children may take many forms. Most of us have an arsenal of techniques and strategies, many of them unconscious, that work to keep our adult children in our sphere of influence. We may operate with a never-ending barrage of judgmental remarks. We may unwittingly give off signs of rejection so minuscule and subtle that they are seldom brought to consciousness by the adult child. We may offer advice in a variety of styles from strongly argumentative to soft-spoken but tenacious. We may do all this and more in the interest of helping our offspring to enter the adult world of responsibility. But we may also be behaving in these ways so as to strengthen our position of control and to weaken our adult child's defenses against it.

We exert control by either threat of punishment or promise of reward. The threat of punishment falls into three major categories: withdrawal of love, of services, or of material support. (We might add to this withdrawal of advice and instruction, although even quite young children reject these much of the time and would not see their withdrawal as punishment.) Similarly, the promise of reward falls into three parallel categories: increase in love, services, or material support. These punishments and rewards are easily recognizable (though not always wise) in the world of parents and young children. We exhibit a stern face or an angry voice (withdrawal of love), we refuse to drive our child to his Little League game (withdrawal of services), or we refuse to buy our daughter a much-wanted outfit (withdrawal of material support). Alternatively, we give him lots of kisses and hugs or a candy bar (increase in love), we offer to mend the hole in his favorite pants (increase in services), or we increase her allowance (increase in material support). Our parenting life is peppered with behaviors like these; they are the stuff of which family life is made.

Can we — and should we — be doing similar, though age-appropriate, things when our children become adults? It seems so easy and so right to continue doing the laundry for our son, a starving grad student living in a crowded flat. And the line is fuzzy between being a helpful parent and being one who manipulates her child into a state of dependence (on the parent) and therefore into a state of low self-esteem. How can we know, for sure, that the need to control is appropriate?

We are caught in the grip of needing to be in control when:

- we act inappropriately uptight or angry over little things, things that don't harm our person or property, (e.g., the way our daughter slurps her soup, our son wearing an earring, nose ring, or tattoo).

- we cannot accept major choices of our adult child regarding education, career, lifestyle, or partner even though these choices do not hurt others.

- we discover, upon reflection, that we are using or withholding love, services, or material support in order to get our adult child to act in ways more acceptable to us.

When we can deeply see, feel, and appreciate the adult status of our children, the need to control evaporates.

The status of adult implies autonomy — that is, freedom to make decisions and enjoy or suffer the consequences of those decisions. When we can deeply see, feel, and appreciate the adult status of our children, the need to control evaporates. We know that our child will make decisions on his own; this is a part of the complex world of adulthood and we applaud and exult in our adult child's membership in that enormous club. Her decisions may not always be the ones we would make but we come to realize that this is part of life. When we reach that stage, the atmosphere is not only fogless but crystal clear. We are free to bask in the sunshine of a relationship of equality.

Letting go of the need to be right

There are many areas of life in which our "rightness" — an attitude we firmly believe to be correct — stands in opposition to others' "wrongness." There are clearly two or more viable points of view. We may "know" we are right, but sooner or later we come upon others who deeply disagree, who find our positions untenable. Some of these others may be our adult children.

Needing to be right in relation to one's adult children is problematic. Our children often don't want us to be right. They are breaking away from us and have been for some time: they want to carve out a life for themselves in the world of young adults. Their choices — what to wear, how to decorate their room, how to spend a vacation — are right for them. In truth, there are no rights and wrongs in aesthetic matters. Yet, even here, where safety, security, or health are not at issue, and where diversity of choice is the rule, we are nevertheless quite capable of feeling that our choices of clothing or hairstyle — both for ourselves and our adult children — are the right ones. Our sense of being right, or of diligently working towards making right decisions, pervades much of our lives. It helps us through difficulties and tight spots, or so we believe. It gives each of us our unique style. And it affects, in an ongoing and profound way, how we raise children.

Can we isolate and describe a point at which "being right" approaches emotional abuse of our adult children? where expressing our views, our sense of what is right, can be called pressure and intimidation? where our willfulness and disinclination to listen to another view nullifies all the gentleness and equality that we have painstakingly developed?

To answer these question it is necessary to distinguish between being right in any given instance and needing to be right. The former hurts no one while the latter is a recipe for alienation. If we can train ourselves to pay attention to our adult children's reaction to our willful expressions of what we believe to be right, we will learn a great deal. It is possible to perceive signs of alienation — sullenness, self-abnegation, pique, unwillingness to focus on the topic at hand — if we are willing to take it in. If our adult child consistently resists listening to us when we have a brilliant perception or draw a staggering conclusion, we are probably correct in regarding our child as alienated from us. Is it abuse? One could argue that it is. But it doesn't help to pin labels on ourselves. More important is to understand the dynamics: our need to be right and our child's need to get out from under the crushing weight of our never being wrong.

It is to everyone's advantage that this painful cycle be broken. One can start by imagining the many different ways — none of them right or wrong in any absolute sense — to eat a meal, to travel to a foreign country, to dress for an outing, to sing a favorite folk song, to word a love letter, or to describe a mountain brook. We are training ourselves in diversity. Our goal is to allow more than one point of view into our universe. We have made a breakthrough if we can say, "I am right, but maybe he is right, too!"

One breakthrough of this sort, if mined for all its treasure, can lead to many others. If we break ground in one area we can envision other, previously opaque, areas of our lives becoming luminescent with possibilities. But the first time we are able to feel and to say to our adult child, "Do what you think best" is the hardest. We are letting go of our need to be right. We are handing our son or daughter the precious gift of their autonomy with our love for them intact. This is no small thing. But at the same time we are getting something in return. We are getting the beginnings of our own true autonomy. We are not passing along automatically to our adult children our received, unquestioned values. We begin to question these values, and in so doing we question ourselves. We begin to sift through what was good and what was not good about our own childhood — the world of good and bad, right and wrong — that our parents laid out for us.

In the real world we are right some of the time and wrong some of the time. More accurately, someone else may have a better solution to a problem than we have come up with. Paradoxically, when we don't need to be right, our thinking is clearer and our judgment more apt. We have more to offer our adult children when we don't need to prove our problem-solving superiority. And there are times when the parents' clear-headedness and years of experience can, indeed, help to turn around the effects of bad decisions on the part of their adult children. But, on balance, letting go of the need to be right relieves the pressure on the parents, reduces resentment of their offspring, and hence allows the great gift of a loving relationship to flourish.

Letting go of the belief that we know more than our adult children

It is tempting to equate age with experience and experience with greater knowledge. We will always be older than our children but we won't always be more experienced or have greater knowledge, understanding, or wisdom. Many people, struggling to survive and doing the best they can, live a routine existence with few attempts to stretch their capabilities or to grow spiritually or intellectually. The experience of having lived, say, 60 years has not expanded their consciousness, given them new, vibrant coping tools, nor afforded them time for travel, study, or other openings to new horizons.

Letting go of the need to be right relieves the pressure on the parents, reduces resentment of their offspring, and hence allows the great gift of a loving relationship to flourish.

It is a provocative thought for many of us that our children may know more than we know. It is easy to accept this if our child is a physicist and we know next to nothing about physics. But it becomes more difficult to accept if our child is a bus driver, a restaurant manager, or a department store clerk. Juggle the idea, for a moment, that your delivery-truck driver son knows more than you ever guessed — about a lot more than company delivery routes. Have you ever discussed social issues with him? Do you know what he knows about home maintenance, gardening, cooking, cars? Do you know what he reads, what he thinks about, what problems he tries to solve? It is certain that applying yourself to this task will punch holes in what might be called the arrogance of age.

Some of you may have grown up in a home where parents trotted out "experience" as an argument against your opinions and ideas. They might have said, "Just wait till you're our age. Then you'll understand what it feels like." It is hard to find a simple rejoinder to this. Since you haven't reached their age, you cannot effectively argue that they are wrong. But the argument from experience is a cheap and unworthy one precisely because it has no ready rejoinder.

It is ironic that midlife (and especially middle class) parents have put a great deal of energy into their children's education as well as the absorption of skills, particularly in sports and the arts. Yet, overall, parents don't want their children to catch up to them. Humility in this area is often not in their bag of tricks. By taking a stance of forever knowing more that their children, parents may feel that they are keeping inviolate their position of authority (and hence their superior status). Their position is both inaccurate and destructive.

Our children very likely inhabit a different knowledge universe than we do. They grew up from babyhood with television in the home (and sometimes in the classroom), electronic typewriters, and later computers. Their medical needs may be addressed with MRIs, CAT scans, and laser technology. Their thinking is informed by a new understanding of toxins, nuclear waste, endangered species, global warming, and other environmental issues which hadn't yet entered into our consciousness when we were their age. We may have some catching up to do.

Letting go of the idea that we know our children better than anyone else does

Knowing our children since birth (or since the age of adoption) seduces us into thinking that we know them better than anyone. How could anyone but parents know the etiology of our young child's minor ailments, emotional upheavals, steps towards maturity, and intellectual growth? As parents, we have collected and catalogued our young child's new words; we know the exact age when he was toilet trained; and, if we haven't saved our child's report cards, most of us have at least collected a vast array of photographs at every stage of his development.

Yet as soon as a child climbs down from our lap he is learning about a world that is not exclusively the world of Mommy and Daddy. When the child attends school, peer activities take on a life of their own. Street-corner sports — shooting hoop in the schoolyard, for example — is a world that parents have no part in. Yet it is a world of powerful friendships and loyal ties, where one's strengths and weaknesses are duly noted and arranged in order of rank by members of the group.

In adolescence, young people have a world of experience that is not shared with parents. These are the years in which one finds one's own identity. Parental models are guides but not blueprints.

Furthermore, the rapidly accelerating social change in the 20th century has produced heretofore unimagined gaps between the generations. Parents do not recognize their offspring, who, in their turn, may not recognize their offspring.

There are real-life consequences when parents persistently think that they know their children better than anyone else:

- Parents may be mired in old "truths" about their children which may have long since disappeared.
- They may be alienating their children by their slightly incorrect responses which don't square with their children's sense of who they are.
- They may not be giving their children a wide enough berth to experiment with new parts of their identity or to grow into more independent people.
- They may be closing themselves off to the real person that is their child right now while fixating on the youngster that they knew back then.

People aren't happy when they are labeled, especially when they are incorrectly labeled. Our children are no exception. They will let Mom and Dad know when their parents' knowledge of them is limited or faulty. This is as it should be; otherwise our children would be denying their experience — always an unhealthy pursuit.

It is incumbent upon us to make frequent reality checks to see where these once small and helpless people whom we still call our children have gone and are going. For some time now they may have found others with whom to share the secrets of their souls. We may not be the ones they come to with inner conflict and turmoil. It may be wise, especially in the case of partnered offspring, to assume that we do not know them best.

Letting go of the need to help

We are all embedded in the social world, surrounded by others who are, at the very least, aware of our existence. It is important to all of us that we know that our death or disappearance would be a loss to some of these others. Depressed individuals live with the conviction that they are alone, isolated — that their death would not affect anything or anyone. Out of this conviction, they feel that they are not needed. Parents have a built-in protection against this in the form of the overwhelming need of babies and small children for nurturing. But this cannot go on indefinitely: it must taper off as the children approach adulthood.

Ideally, we would like to be pleased to see our adult children succeed. But success implies independence, and independence implies ability to cope, mastering of marketable skills, and financial stability. Our children need our help less as they succeed as adults. With a little probing we may discover in ourselves a measure of fear of our children's success. Denying that fear will push it underground, while facing it is the first step to expunging it. Paradoxically, it is benign for a parent to be available to his or her children for help, but that helping hand can become toxic when the parent needs to be needed.

Paradoxically, it is benign for a parent to be available to his or her children for help, but that helping hand can become toxic when the parent needs to be needed.

Similar to, but not identical with, the scheme of rewards and punishments outlined above, are the three categories of help we offer our adult children: advice, services, and money. If a parent doesn't have services or money to offer, advice can always be summoned up. For some, giving advice doesn't stop with the children. It extends to other family members and friends and is an ongoing interpersonal strategy. The need to be needed (and its extension, the need to help) is a powerful, lifelong, motivating force for many. It appears to have the magic to ward off demons. And it calls up the sweet words — "thank you."

When we begin to let go of the need to help our adult children, we are on the track of actually helping them. For the first time we may listen to them without interjecting our experienced, parental selves into the interaction. By really listening, we come to know when our well-intentioned advice is felt by them to be an insult. By simply listening, we are letting our adult children know that we love them and that they don't have to earn our love. And we glimpse the idea that we may be helping most, paradoxically, by not helping at all.

Letting go of the feeling of responsibility for
our children's success or happiness

If one of parents' secret wishes is that their children will go on need-ing them forever, another may be that their child's success and happiness has been and still is the parents' doing. Obsession with our role in our children's success and happiness is a state of bondage. It is time to let go of this enormous weight.

We have given our adult children our blessing but often that blessing is less an outright gift than a long thread with attachments on it. We send messages along this thread whenever we deem it necessary. If our adult child is happy and successful, we can sit back and relax, exulting in the good results of all of our hard parenting work. If our child is unable to cope or on the edge, we will surely search for some clear and cogent reasons for this, and then try to resolve the problem.

It is exceedingly difficult to divorce ourselves from the feeling of being responsible in the first place. Our children don't stop being our children just because they have grown up, a cliché that our own par-ents impressed upon us and which turns out to be true. Furthermore, their happiness reflects on us — or does it? One of the most therapeu-tic steps we can take in this regard is to insert a wedge in the steel bond that connects parent and child. Or, to use the image described above, to cut the long thread with attachments on it. To imagine our child, every once in a while, as just another person.

Just as our child's problems are his problems, not ours, his suc-cess is his own, not ours. If we have taken his success and happiness to heart, making it ours, it is time to give it back to him. Shouldering his problems is a burden. But reveling in his success is equally a burden, if we consider that, should he no longer be successful, we will very like-ly revert back to our earlier worry and self-castigation.

It is important to reflect on the multiple definitions of success. The world of advertising lures us into thinking of the Mercedes Benz owner as more successful than the owner of a ten-year-old Honda: Our brains become clouded by commercial hype. Instead, you might con-sider the following criteria as indications of success. Our children are successful if they can:

- live within their income,
- avoid credit card debt,
- avoid craving everything in sight,
- feel they have discovered an occupation, activity, or pastime that they love,
- are able to withhold gratification and to save up for something desirable, beautiful, or lasting,
- call on loyal friends who support them and love them.

Finally, our children's lack of success by any definition, even their chronic unhappiness and continual bad times, still belongs to them, not to us. They have to figure out how to climb out of the morass they are in and to make the most of their strengths. And we have to learn how to measure incremental gains appropriate to each child. A first step taken by a long-bedridden accident victim is a major success.

Letting go of our expectations of how our adult children should live

The story is told that George Frederic Handel's father wanted his son to become a lawyer, not a composer. Young George had to write his eloquent music late at night in the attic, on the sly. He entered law school to please his father, but soon left to play in an orchestra in Hamburg, where he composed his earliest operas. Listening to Handel's music, we have no clue to the suffering he may have gone through until he was able to pursue his musical destiny.

The power of parental disapproval can be devastating to the child who cannot or will not live a lie. It may be even more catastrophic to the one who gives in to parental expectations. It extends to many areas besides choice of occupation and feeds the flames of lifetime resentment and coldness between parent and adult child.

Desire for their adult children's success and happiness is not the only thing parents may crave. They may also want their children to look "right," to speak "right," and to have the "right" home, the "right" friends, the "right" politics and values. How does our son's long hair, nose ring, or tattoo reflect on us, his parents? We may have great difficulty letting go of revulsion towards unfamiliar grooming and lifestyle habits in our sons and daughters, and the nagging feeling that their traits make us look bad. Such a feeling is testament to the fact that our adult children have considerable power over us. It is time to let our daughter's pink hair just be part of the passing parade. There are others like her, and probably other offended, uncomfortable parents. Midlife parents have too much living yet to do to waste precious minutes attempting to change the looks and behavior of their adult children to approximate those of an older generation.

Letting go of our expectations of how parents and adult children should relate

> *Around the holidays, unresolved family issues tend to get hotter than a pan of jewel yams. Children carry the memory of hurt or anger from family relationships well into adulthood. Many people stay away from their parents or visit them reluctantly, bracing themselves to swallow, ignore, or fight over issues that have haunted them for years.*[3]
>
> — *Joshua Coleman in "Strangers at Our Table,"* San Fransisco Chronicle

It is time to re-think the notion that our adult children should be at our festive table on Thanksgiving. The problem with Thanksgiving, as with all holidays, is that it prods our interaction into certain preconceived patterns. It is possible to get so wrapped up in the Thanksgiving formula (or the Christmas, New Year's, or even birthday formulas) that we forget what is going on in the here-and-now with our adult children. If we do not allow for deviation from the formula or if we fail to anticipate change, we will probably experience conflict and pain.

It is wise to avoid letting holidays dominate our thinking and our behavior. If the chief point of that quintessential American holiday, Thanksgiving, is the experience of warmth and togetherness with one's family, then surely we can set up days of thanksgiving at any time. We can ask our children if they would like to celebrate the first day of spring with us, or the new moon, or the last day of school, or the day we send in our income tax. And there is nothing to prevent us from giving thanks, any time and any place, for the things in our lives which really touch us.

Besides creating holidays to celebrate, we can also devise new ways to celebrate traditional holidays. Independence Day can be the backdrop for a scavenger hunt in which adults and children can participate equally. Thanksgiving and Christmas can serve as times for giving to others in the community — baked goods and toys, for example.

Most importantly, we can work jointly with our adult children to plan a celebration. Instead of saying, "We're having a family party on New Year's Day and we'd like you to come," we can say instead, "Would you like to do something with us on New Year's Day? We're open to suggestions." Our children may already be committed for that day. So be it. Another day will work out just as well.

Linda Ellerbee, in an article in *New Choices* magazine, came up with the following speech when her daughter announced that she wasn't coming home for Christmas: "It's perfectly fine for you to enjoy Christmas in Seattle. We'll miss you, but I understand. What I don't want is to have to go through this every year. Me wondering: Is she coming home this Christmas? You wondering: What will Mom think if I don't come home? We both deserve better, so I have an idea. From now on, we'll have a big family Christmas *every other* year. On the odd years, I'll go skiing, you do what you want, and nobody's feelings will get tangled."[4]

Thinking about letting go of old relationship rules may also start parents thinking about what they don't want to give up — what rules and behaviors are inviolable. If parents discover that they have a bottom-line need for civility (please, thank you, excuse me, etc.), they should communicate this clearly to their children. If, on the other hand, parents' bottom-line is fairly regular letter writing, e-mailing, or phoning, this too needs to be stated. But if children forget to phone, parents may have to be prepared either to do without regular communication or to initiate it themselves.

Letting go and selfishness

Parents don't want to be, or to appear to be, selfish. Even though they may say, "Don't bother me; can't you see I'm busy?" they would like their behaviour to be seen as justified and excusable. The parents' busyness is simply more important than the kids' intrusion. The parents' needs and the children's needs do not always have equal status. Parents see their needs for rest, recreation, and stimulation as legitimate — and work hard at presenting them as such to the world. If these needs are legitimate, then they, the parents, are not selfish.

Selfishness is not synonymous with letting go, but there is an important link between the two — our old enemy, guilt. If a parent can guiltlessly think of her non-parenting needs (e.g., travel, education, career training, music lessons, etc.) as legitimate, then letting go is substantially easier. Guilt makes us deny selfishness. We cannot comfortably give up power if an awareness of the selfishness of our desires keeps threatening to break through into our consciousness and if we cannot accept that selfishness in ourselves. We cannot (we think) be a good parent and be selfish at the same time. "Unacceptable" selfishness triggers a reaction: We need to become Supermom or Superdad, ready with up-to-the-minute, how-to advice, available at all hours for transportation and all manner of other services, ready and willing to fund our children's education, sports, travel, cars, and even homes.

Coming at this from another angle, letting go of the burden of guilt opens us up to being more altruistic. Does this mean that we will be less involved in our own activities if we let go, and more willing to do things for our children? Not exactly. It does mean that we are less likely to be burdened with the need to be perfect parents. We are no longer being called upon to raise our adult children: they have been raised and now it is up to them. While letting go gives us more time to follow our own pursuits, paradoxically our minds and hearts are freer, less burdened with over-identification, less concerned with possible loss of status, less worried about appearances. As a result, a generosity of spirit will emanate from us that will be felt by everyone around us — most significantly, by our children.

We cannot achieve the calmness that we are seeking by simply determining to be more selfish, by adopting a "healthy" attitude toward self-fulfillment, or by benignly neglecting our adult child in order to get to the letting-go goal post. It is never a straight shot, and certainly not a simple one. There are obstacles along the path that require that we make choices. Awareness and attention to detail need to become part of our basic life equipment.

Letting go and aging

It is very cathartic to be able to say honestly, "I really don't care who my child marries, what my child works at, how my child lives — as long as she's happy." This high-minded position breaks down, however, when our child appears to be unhappy. Then we feel justified in stepping in, calling upon all of our old habits of worrying, advising, and over-identifying. In the process, we also bring out into the open our half-buried prejudices regarding the "right" kind of spouse, a "good" job, a "sensible" life-style.

If we genuinely don't mind how our child lives as long as she's happy, we may have to accept our child's homosexuality. For some, this is a challenge, a test. If we stick with our conviction that homosexuality is bad, then our homosexual child must be bad. Defending our position is a form of flunking the test. This serves no one and will only bring pain to our families.

But an even greater test presents itself when we are called upon to accept the child who is in serious jeopardy: a son in jail, a daughter who has taken up prostitution, an alcoholic child, or a heroine addict. Our desire to reject our child out of hand does battle with our guilt at having caused his problems. In either case, we cannot take a calm and easy approach to it all. And yet here, especially here, letting go may be the only way to achieve adult/adult friendship with our children.

Living out our lives in a state of self-blame helps no one. If we live to be 90 and beyond we may let go by default because we are busy attending to our medical needs or experiencing memory loss. Some elderly people worry less and less because they can't remember what it is that they're supposed to worry about. But if we can stop worrying, let go, and connect lovingly with our adult children during our midlife years, we will have many more years to enjoy our relationship. Waiting until self-absorption is thrust upon us denies the possibility that we can develop an egalitarian friendship with our adult child when we are in the prime of life. Such a friendship is not only possible, it can be one of the great joys of the midlife years.

Letting go as experienced by our adult children

Adult children need to help their parents to let go by instructing them in what needs to be done. Parents, even with the best of intentions, can't always make the first move. Relinquishing power and control takes strength and courage. It may be accompanied by a sense of diminishment and by feelings of guilt at not properly performing our role as parent. We may feel our child needs our guidance. We may feel he can't do X, Y, or Z without us. We see him as disorganized and benefiting from our ability to prioritize or to see things clearly.

Adult children can sometimes show their parents the way. Your daughter might tell you, "Both of us will be happier if you lay off trying to improve me." Your son might remind you, "If I need your help, I'll ask you for it." Either of these statements may be felt by parents as a slap in the face: they seem to be saying, "I don't need you anymore." Adult children are wise if they can give these and similar messages clearly, without rancor or resentment. Most parents know full well that they are not needed as much anymore, but they may be trying to delay the inevitable. Savor a message from your adult child that lets you know, "I don't need you very much anymore but I still love you and you are still part of my life." Consider yourself blessed to receive such a message. Use it as a starting point for letting go.

The challenges for parents:

- to let go gracefully of the power mandate you have exercised all these years regarding your children.
- to practice saying to your adult children, "Do what you think best."
- to explore the ways you use the reward/punishment mechanisms of control.
- to understand the difference between being right in any given instance and needing to be right.

- to entertain the thought that your adult children may be wiser and/or more knowledgeable than you.
- to recognize that your need to help may get in the way of actually helping your children.
- to give your child's successes back to him if you have appropriated them for yourself.
- to think about the different ways to measure success.
- to find new ways to celebrate with your family, thus eliminating behavioral molds that don't work.
- to begin to let go of your children while you are still young enough to enjoy your freedom.
- to recognize that letting go of your adult children does not necessarily mean that they will leave. On the contrary, they are likely to want to spend more time with the new you.

Endnotes

CHAPTER 1. GETTING TO KNOW EACH OTHER:
The Parallel Worlds of Parents and Adult Children

1. J.M.Coetzee, *Disgrace*, (Penguin Books, 1999), p. 86.
2. The statistics in Chapter 1 were collected from infoplease.com and come from a variety of sources including United Nations Demographic Yearbook, 1997; World Population Profile, 1998; United States Census Bureau; Department of Health and Human Services, National Center for Health Statistics, <www.dhhs.gov>.

CHAPTER 2. SPEAKING FROM THE HEART:
Communicating With Your Adult Children

1. See Sylvia Boorstein, *It's Easier Than You Think*, (HarperSanFrancisco, 1995), p. 49.
2. C. Flax and E. Ubell, *Mother/Father/You: An Adult's Guide for Getting Along Great With Parents and In-laws*, (Wyden Books, 1980), p. 78.
3. ibid., p. 151.
4. E. Goffman, *The Presentation of Self in Everyday Life*, (Doubleday Anchor, 1959), p. 217.
5. S. Jonas and M. Nissenson, *Friends for Life: Enriching the Bond Between Mothers and Their Adult Daughters*, (William Morrow, 1997), p. 343.
6. Flax and Ubell, op.cit., p. 60.
7. Erving Goffman elaborates on the theme of "protecting the role of the other" in a number of his writings. This quote is from "On Face-Work, An Analysis of Ritual Elements in Social Interaction", *Interaction Ritual: Essays on Face-to-Face Behavior*, (Anchor, 1967), p. 29. "One common type of tacit co-operation in face-saving is the tact exerted in regard to face-work itself. The person not only defends his own face and protects the face of the others, but also acts so as to make it possible and even easy for the others to employ face-work for themselves and him. He helps them to help themselves and him."

CHAPTER 4. SELF-DEVELOPMENT:
A Path to Friendship With Your Adult Child

1. S. Levine, *Who Dies? An Investigation of Conscious Living and Conscious Dying*, (Anchor Books, 1982), p. 70.

2. The Serenity Prayer is attributed to theologian Reinhold Niebhr, who is supposed to have composed it in 1932 as part of a longer prayer. Besides being used at AA meetings, it was distributed to hundreds of thousands of servicemen in World War II and became enormously popular. Niebuhr published it in a column in 1951 but it was never copyrighted. See Richard Fox, *Reinhold Niebuhr, A Biography*, (Harper & Row, 1985), pp. 209-210.

3. Erving Goffman, in his provocative book, *Stigma*, deconstructs the many-faceted, often devastating effects on a person with a physical and visible trait that is deemed inferior and that cannot be hidden. He quotes from a psychiatric journal. See H.S. Perry, M.L. Gawel, and M. Gibbon, eds., *Clinical Studies in Psychiatry*, Norton & Co, 1956), p. 145; quoted in E. Goffman, *Stigma*, (Prentice-Hall, 1963), p. 13. "The awareness of inferiority means that one is unable to keep out of consciousness the formulation of some chronic feeling of the worst sort of insecurity. The fear that others can disrespect a person because of something he shows means that he is always insecure in his contact with other people...that represents an almost fatal deficiency of the self-system since the self is unable to disguise or exclude a definite formulation that reads, 'I am inferior. Therefore people will dislike me and I cannot be secure with them.'"

4. G.K. Chesterton, quoted in R.D. Laing, *The Politics of Experience*, (Pantheon Books, 1967), p. 86.

5. William Shakespeare, *The Merchant of Venice*, Act 4, Scene 1.

6. Written during World War II, Fromm's book addresses the psychological underpinnings of the acceptance of submission to authority in the West during this period. He shows that the idea of freedom has changed over time, and that in the post-industrial period, we have a new mandate. See E. Fromm, *Escape From Freedom* (Holt, Rinehart & Winston, 1941, reprinted in Avon Books, 1965), p.126. "although each of the liberties which have been won must be defended with utmost vigor, the problem of freedom is not only a quantitative one, but a qualitative one; that we

not only have to preserve and increase the traditional freedom, but that we have to gain a new kind of freedom, one which enables us to realize our own individual self, to have faith in this self and in life."

CHAPTER 5. CRISES:
When Something Goes Wrong in Your Adult Child's Life

1. E. Maisel, 20 *Communication Tips For Families*, (New World Library, 2000), pp. 2-3.
2. M. Caplan, *When Sons and Daughters Choose Alternative Lifestyles*, (Hohm Press, 1996), p. 111.
3. ibid., pp. 111-112.
4. S. Levine, op.cit., p. 202.

CHAPTER 6. SHARING:
Erasing the Barriers to Engagement Between You and Your Child

1. Rainer Maria Rilke, *Sonnets to Orpheus*, part II, no. 1, trans. C.F. MacIntire (University of California Press, 1960), p. 57.

CHAPTER 7. INDEPENDENCE:
The Competing Needs of Parents and Adult Children

1. E. Maisel, op.cit., pp. 19-20.
2. See, for example, C.H. Cooley, *Social Organization* (Scribners, 1909). The following short description of Cooley's primary group/secondary group formulation may be found in *Aspects of Sociology*, authored by The Frankfurt Institute for Social Research, (Beacon Press, 1972), p. 58. "Cooley emphasizes the importance of small human groups, the family, play groups, or groups of neighbors; he has given formations of this sort [the] term primary groups, because they are primary in time as well as in their significance for the individual, in the development of the personality and the preservation of social conceptions and ideals, when compared to the secondary groups, among which Cooley includes such groupings as the state, party, class, etc."

CHAPTER 8. GRANDPARENTING:
A Fresh Look for the New Millennium

1. Z. Schachter-Shalomi and R.S. Miller, *From Age-ing to Sage-ing: a Profound New Vision of Growing Older*, (Warner Books, 1995), p. 204.

CHAPTER 9. THE CHALLENGE OF THE FUTURE:
Growing into Mature Relationship With Your Adult Children

1. Flax and Ubell, op.cit., p. 10
2. Jonas and Nissenson, op.cit., p. 344.
3. Joshua Coleman, "Strangers at Our Table", *San Francisco Chronicle*, Nov. 12, 2000, p. 4.
4. Linda Ellerbee, "Linda Ellerbee's Holiday Miracle," *New Choices*, Dec. 1996 - Jan. 1997, p. 33.

Bibliography

Alter, Robert M., and Jane Alter. *The Transformative Power of Crisis: Our Journey to Psychological Healing and Psychological Awakening.* New York: ReganBooks, Div. HarperCollins, 2000.

Berne, Eric. *Games People Play: The Psychology of Human Relationships.* New Relationships. New York: Ballantine Books, 1964.

Bloomfield, Harold. *Making Peace With Your Parents.* New York: Random House, 1983.

Boorstein, Sylvia. *It's Easier Than You Think.* HarperSanFrancisco, 1995.

Brody, Elaine. *Women in the Middle: Their Parent-Care Years.* New York: Springer Publishing, 1990.

Bryan, Mark. *Codes of Love.* New York: Pocket Books, 1999.

Caplan, Mariana. *When Sons and Daughters Choose Alternative Lifestyles.* Prescott, AZ: Hohm Press, 1996.

Carlson, Kathie. *In Her Image: The Unhealed Daughter's Search for Her Mother.* Boston & London: Shambhala Publications, 1990.

Carlson, Richard. *Don't Sweat the Small Stuff — and It's All Small Stuff* New York: Hyperion, 1997.

Coetzee, J.M. *Disgrace.* New York: Penguin Books, 1999.

Corneau, Guy. *Absent Fathers, Lost Sons: The Search for Masculine Identity.* Boston & London: Shambhala Publications, 1991.

Feuerstein, Phyllis and Carol Roberts. *The Not-So-Empty Nest: How to Live With Your Kids After They've Lived Someplace Else.* Chicago: Follet, 1981.

Fischer, Lucy. *Linked Lives: Adult Daughters and Their Mothers.* New York: Harper and Row, 1986.

Flax, Carol C. and Earl Ubell. *Mother/Father/You: An Adult's Guide for Getting Along Great with Parents and In-laws.* New York: Wyden Books, 1980.

Forward, Susan. *Emotional Blackmail.* New York: HarperCollins, 1997.

Fox, Richard. *Reinhold Niebuhr, A Biography.* San Francisco: Harper & Row, 1985.

Frain, Betty and Eileen M. Clegg. *Becoming a Wise Parent For Your Grown Child*. Oakland, CA: New Harbinger Publications, 1997.

Frankfurt Institute for Social Research. *Aspects of Sociology*. Boston: Beacon Press, 1972.

Fromm, Erich. *Escape From Freedom*. Holt, Rinehart & Winston, 1941.

Galinsky, Ellen. *The Six Stages of Parenthood*. Reading, MA: Addison-Wesley, 1987.

Goffman, Erving. *Interaction Ritual: Essays on Face-to-Face Behavior*. New York: Anchor, 1967.

——————— *The Presentation of Self in Everyday Life*. Garden City, NY: Doubleday Anchor, 1959.

——————— *Stigma*. Englewood Cliffs, N.J.: Prentice-Hall, 1963.

Graves, C. and Stockman, L.V. *Adult Children Who Won't Grow Up*. Chicago: Contemporary Books, 1989.

Greenberg, Vivian E. *Your Best is Good Enough: Aging Parents and Your Emotions*. New York: Lexington Books, 1989.

Gross, Zenith H. *And You Thought it Was All Over: Mothers and Their Adult Children*. New York: St. Martin's/Marek, 1985.

Harris, Amy B. and Thomas Harris. *Staying OK*. New York: Harper and Row, 1985.

Harris, Thomas. *I'm OK — You're OK*. New York: Avon Books, 1967.

Higgins, Gina O. *Resilient Adults Overcoming a Cruel Past*. San Fransisco: Jossey-Bass Publishers, 1994.

Horney, Karen. *Self-Analysis*. New York — London: W.W. Norton, 1942.

Jampolsky, Gerald G. *Teach Only Love: The Seven Principles of Attitudinal Healing*. New York: Bantam, 1983.

Jonas, Susan, and Marilyn Nissenson. *Friends For Life: Enriching the Bond Between Mothers and Their Adult Daughters*. New York: William Morrow, 1997.

Koch, Thomas. *Mirrored Lives: Aging Children and Elderly Parents*. New York: Praeger, 1990.

Kornfield, Jack. *A Path With Heart: A Guide Through the Perils and Promises of Spiritual Life*. New York: Bantam Books, 1993.

Laing, R.D. *The Politics of Experience*. New York: Pantheon Books, 1967.

Levine, Stephen. *Who Dies? An Investigation of Conscious Living and Conscious Dying.* Garden City, NY: Anchor Books, 1982.

Lieber, Phyllis, Gloria S. Murphy and Annette M. Schwartz. *Grown up Children, Grown up Parents: Opening the Door to Healthy Relationships Between Parents and Adult Children.* Secaucus, NJ: Carol Publishing Group, 1994.

Littwin, Susan. *The Postponed Generation: Why American Youth Are Growing up LATER.* New York: William Morrow, 1986.

Maisel, Eric. *20 Communication Tips for Families.* Novato, CA: New World Library, 2000.

Maslow, Arthur and Moira Duggan. *Family Connections: Parenting Your Grown Children.* New York: Doubleday, 1982.

Okimoto, J.D. and P.J. Stegall. *Boomerang Kids.* Boston: Little Brown, 1987.

Rilke, Rainer Maria. *Sonnets to Orpheus.* Trans. C.F. MacIntire. Berkeley, Los Angeles, London: University of California Press, 1960.

Schachter-Shalomi, Zalman, and Ronald S. Miller. *From Age-ing to Sage-ing: A Profound New Vision of Growing Older.* New York: Warner Books, 1995.

Secunda, Victoria. *When You and Your Mother Can't Be Friends.* New York: Delacorte Press, 1990.

Shapiro, Patricia G. *My Turn: Women's Search for Self After the Children Leave.* Princeton, NJ: Peterson's, 1996.

Smith, Shauna. *Making Peace With Your Adult Children.* New York: Plenum Press, 1991.

Unell, Barbara C., and Jerry L. Wycoff. *The 8 Seasons of Parenthood.* New York: Times Books, 2000.

Viorst, Judith. *Necessary Losses.* New York: Simon and Schuster, 1986.

Weinstock, Nicholas. *The Secret Love of Sons.* New York: Riverhead Books, 1997.

York, Phyllis, David York, and Ted Wachtel. *Toughlove Solutions.* New York: Doubleday, 1984.

About the Author

ROBERTA MAISEL is a volunteer mediator with Berkeley Dispute Resolution Service in Berkeley, California. She is an enthusiastic parent of three grown children and, at various times in her life, has been a school teacher, antique shop owner, piano accompanist, and political activist working with and for Central American refugees, homeless people and Middle East peace.

Born in New York City, Roberta received a B.A. from Brandeis and an M.A. in Sociology from UC Berkeley, and had a brief stint teaching at the college level. More recently she has given talks and workshops on aging, living with loss, and getting along with adult children. When she became widowed in 1993 at the age of 58, her life changed direction and she found what she thinks of as a new calling — writing. Her children have been a deep source of inspiration and insight.

If you have enjoyed *All Grown Up*, you might also enjoy other

BOOKS TO BUILD A NEW SOCIETY

Our books provide positive solutions for people who want to
make a difference. We specialize in:

Educational and Parenting Resources • Nonviolence
Sustainable Living • Ecological Design and Planning
Natural Building & Appropriate Technology • New Forestry
Environment and Justice • Conscientious Commerce
Progressive Leadership • Resistance and Community

For a full list of NSP's titles, please call **1-800-567-6772** *or check out our web site at:*

www.newsociety.com

NEW SOCIETY PUBLISHERS